D1454538

The Observer's Pocket Series

MOTOR SPORT

THE OBSERVER BOOKS

A POCKET REFERENCE SERIES COVERING A WIDE RANGE OF SUBJECTS

Natural History
BIRDS
BIRD'S EGGS
BUTTERFLIES
LARGER MOTHS
COMMON INSECTS
WILD ANIMALS
ZOO ANIMALS
WILD FLOWERS
GARDEN FLOWERS
FLOWERING TREES
  AND SHRUBS
HOUSE PLANTS
CACTI
TREES
GRASSES
COMMON FUNGI
LICHENS
POND LIFE
FRESHWATER FISHES
SEA FISHES
SEA AND SEASHORE
GEOLOGY
ASTRONOMY
WEATHER
CATS
DOGS
HORSES AND PONIES

Transport
AIRCRAFT
AUTOMOBILES
COMMERCIAL VEHICLES

SHIPS
MANNED SPACEFLIGHT
UNMANNED SPACEFLIGHT
BRITISH STEAM
  LOCOMOTIVES

The Arts, etc.
ARCHITECTURE
CATHEDRALS
CHURCHES
HERALDRY
FLAGS
PAINTING
MODERN ART
SCULPTURE
FURNITURE
MUSIC
POSTAGE STAMPS
POTTERY AND PORCELAIN
BRITISH AWARDS AND
  MEDALS
EUROPEAN COSTUME
SEWING

Sport
ASSOCIATION FOOTBALL
CRICKET
GOLF
MOTOR SPORT

Cities
LONDON

The Observer's Book of
MOTOR SPORT

GRAHAM MACBETH

WITH 57 BLACK AND WHITE
PHOTOGRAPHS
AND 39 DIAGRAMS

FREDERICK WARNE & CO LTD

FREDERICK WARNE & CO INC

LONDON . NEW YORK

ACKNOWLEDGEMENTS

The author and publishers wish to thank the following for their kind permission to reproduce photographs: Embassy Racing Press Office, page 7; Autocar, pages 25, 26, 32, 37, 39, 54, 55, 81, 83 (all), 85 (all), 87 (all), 114 (both), 116 (right) and 119 (right); National Motor Museum, pages 31, 33, 35, 113 (both) and 119 (left); London Art Tech, pages 45, 56, 62, 67, 68, 69, 70, 72, 75 (both), 76, 77, 108, 116 (left), 117 (both), 120 (both), 123 (right) and 177; John Player & Sons, pages 88 and 125; The Press Association Ltd, page 121 (right); Ford Motor Co Ltd, pages 121 (left), 123 (left), 124 (both) and 173; Alexander Duckham & Co Ltd, page 179.

Library of Congress Catalog
Card No. 73–93586

ISBN 0 7232 1530 8

Printed in Great Britain by
Butler & Tanner Limited
Frome and London

512.775

CONTENTS

PREFACE

Motor sport has been taking some hard knocks recently. The world oil crisis resulting from the action of Arab countries following the 1973 Egyptian/Syrian/Israeli war has meant that some people, who might otherwise not have thought much about it, have attacked motor racing and rallying, and the various other forms of motor sport, as being entirely unnecessary and wasteful activities. Motor sport has been accused of being anti-social towards people in general as well as dangerous for the participants.

These opinions have been challenged effectively by those who support motor sport and this must be a suitable time for a new book which sets out, comprehensively, the past record and present situation of this sport, so that those who discuss it can, at least, have an additional opportunity of hearing what it is all about.

That is one possible use for this book. For most people, however, it is intended to be nothing more than a compact survey of a sport of consuming passion to many people and of great attraction to very many more, a substantial majority of whom may welcome this opportunity to become better informed about this very complex subject.

If it adds a few hours of extra enjoyment to the lives of each follower of motor sport who reads it, the effort of writing this book will have been well worth while.

FOREWORD
by Graham Hill,
O.B.E.

In Great Britain, motor racing has been supported by an ever-expanding number of enthusiasts for the whole of the period during which I, personally, have been involved in the sport. Yet I know that there are vast numbers of people who are just on the fringe of this enthusiasm, who like watching the occasional motor race but don't necessarily enjoy it as much as they could because they don't have sufficient understanding of what is involved. The same must apply to the many other forms of motor sport such as rallying and autocross. This book should sort all that out. It is a small book but I can't think of anything else comparable in price or size which packs in so much information.

Obviously, I am biased in approving of the fact that motor racing gets the lion's share of the space. In recent years, it has become a great and world-wide industry as well as a sport. It is very costly and highly professional, but it is still a sport. At least among the drivers, I know of nobody who participates without doing so primarily because they enjoy it. Their enjoyment is reflected by the quite staggering enthusiasm being generated in places such as Brazil and Argentina, where magnificent new race circuits are being built and where motor racing now seems to rival football in public excitement.

About the author. When I first got to know Graham Macbeth, it was as a race organizer rather than a journalist and I always seemed to find my entrants arguing with him over my starting money. He must have been the meanest organizer of them all and I can't think why I'm now writing the foreword for his book! To be charitable, I know he was doing his best for the people whose races he was organizing. I don't think we ever fell out entirely.

I wish him every success with this book and I commend it to you, the reader.

INTRODUCTION

Since the motor car became available to more than the very few pioneer constructor/drivers, there has been motor sport in some form or another.

It is generally agreed that the first effective motor cars were not made until the late 1880s, yet the first recorded organized motor competition took place in 1894. From then on, races and trials took place regularly. There is little doubt that drivers of the very early cars vied with each other in unofficial contests to prove the superiority of their own machines, for man is essentially a competitive animal.

It was only natural that the attitudes which sustained a highly organized horse-racing industry in the late 19th and early 20th centuries should generate competition between men and their powered machines, especially when it became clear that these could provide a level of performance comparable with that of the hitherto unchallenged steam train. What is more, this speed was combined with an independence denied to any device running on rails.

Motor sport sets out to achieve a variety of aims. It is a combined challenge to both man and machine. It can be claimed, with complete justification, that it improves the cars which are used to compete and the many components associated with them. It is a way in which one man can pit his ability – to control a car, to cover a distance, to get to the top of a hill – against that of others.

It is a sport which is almost without bounds. It thrives in the Western world, with maximum activity in Europe and North America. It is widespread in all other parts of America, and in Australasia, Africa, the Middle East and most parts of the Far East.

On a limited scale, it also takes place within the Communist countries, with various forms of racing and rallying in Russia, Poland and Czechoslovakia. Of the world's major countries, only China does not seem to have organized motor sport, but on its very borders, in Hong Kong and Macao, there is tremendous enthusiasm for the local race meetings.

Because of the speeds involved, motor sport is essentially a dangerous activity. The spirit of competition encourages virtually all participants to drive their cars at very close to their limits of ability. Sometimes, the unexpected occurs so that, temporarily, the speed is beyond the limit and then accidents occur. Often, they result in nothing more serious than some minor damage to the cars. Occasionally, they are sufficiently serious to result in the death of one or more of the participants and, just possibly, even of the onlookers.

Paradoxically, this danger which results from speed getting beyond control has invested motor sport with a glamour which is additional to the attraction of speed and competition alone. The glamour stems, too, from the fact that motor sport tends to be expensive to a greater or lesser degree. In consequence, those who participate are involved with a relatively high degree of wealth, even if they do not possess any of it themselves. Thus drivers who may achieve only minimal success will choose motor sport as a profession even when they may know that they could earn a better living in other ways, and racing mechanics put up with incredibly long working hours and inferior working conditions for less than they would receive at a regular $5\frac{1}{2}$ day-week job at their local garage.

Over the years, motor sport has become, for many, a matter of national pride and prestige, over and above that developed by companies and individuals. This reached its height in the days between the wars, when the German government used Grand Prix motor racing as a national prestige exercise with huge financial grants from exchequer to car builder (Mercedes-Benz and Auto-Union). The German cars dominated their racing with near-complete success, these two teams spending most of their time in direct competition with each other, leaving the rest of the field far behind.

Although there have been no similar examples of Government intervention of this type since, there have been many subsequent efforts by car makers and private teams in which national pride has been a major incentive. In these days, it is the Japanese who use motor competition directly to boost car sales on an international basis.

While many will regard national pride as laudable, the pressures which it causes in motor sport have occasionally been proved to be unbearably great. Men have literally driven themselves to their deaths because they felt that they were driving for their mother country. It is likely that such great drivers as Bernd Rosemeyer of Germany and Eugenio Castellotti of Italy would not have met the deaths that they did, but for their intense patriotism which urged them on at moments demanding caution. Rosemeyer crashed on a dangerously windy day in a record-breaking attempt, while Castelotti was killed while trying to challenge the opposition in a clearly outpaced car. These are extreme cases, but there is no doubt that many other drivers have taken extra chances because they were aware that the eyes of their countrymen were upon them and because they felt that a supreme effort was needed to keep their national flag flying high.

On a lower scale, there is a 'hungryness' which makes some drivers shine out above the rest. The urge to climb further up the ladder of success is immensely strong in some people, and in motor sport it can produce a degree of ruthlessness which goes far beyond the bounds of normal enthusiasm. When combined with skill it will often result in the more ruthless driver winning, all other things being equal. He will be the last man of a bunch to brake on the entrance to a corner in a race, or the one who slows least on the most difficult parts of a rally special stage. His rivals will regard him with mixed feelings of awe and suspicion, aware that such people have more and worse accidents than the majority and that they may frequently involve others. Very closely matched types of cars demonstrate this situation most clearly with Formula Ford and Formula 3 races giving many examples. The usual incident is for a bunch of perhaps half-a-dozen cars in a scrap for the lead, with two or three 'hungry' lads among equally skilled but perhaps not quite so determined rivals. One of the 'hungry' ones leaves his braking a fraction too late and, momentarily, the car is not quite in control. The situation would be retrieved by the skill of the others but for the fact that another 'hungry' one is also slightly over the limit. They touch and, in a fraction of a second, there are cars spinning all over the track, wheels and suspensions tearing off and flying in the air, and an immense problem has materialized in a moment for the next pack of cars following close behind.

Amazingly, most such incidents result in little more than expensive but quite easily repairable damage to the cars, a few bruises for the driver and some additional tarnish to reputations. Motor racing authority is not particularly effective in curbing the activities of such people and, mostly, they grow out of the worst stages of their ruthlessness with greater experience.

All competition drivers take calculated risks but the 'hungry' ones are prepared to calculate their odds to a much narrower limit. Where the form of competition keeps the cars apart, as in sprints, hill-climbs and, to a certain extent, rallies, ruthlessness is likely to show as no more than a higher incidence of accidents so that the driver concerned is likely to run out of funds or support.

Unlike most other forms of sport, there is very seldom any distinction between amateur or pro-fessional drivers. Occasionally, there will be special awards for private entrants but, for the most part, drivers are just competitors. He who can obtain the best equipment, either because he has the funds of his own, or is recognized by others as being suffi-ciently able to warrant support, goes ahead and gets the best cars or engines. Nobody begrudges this or cares whether he earns his living by driving a com-petition car or serving behind a bank counter.

In practice, the majority of drivers in the lowest levels of motor sport – club rallies, minor autocross events and the smallest race meetings, for instance – are amateur. In the upper regions of the sport, Grand Prix racing and international rallying, there are very few who are not wholly professional. The reasons are simple. Nobody is going to pay a driver to take part in a club rally or run at the back of a field in a race confined to Minis, while the driver who works in the motor trade and uses one of his firm's cars to go on a rally is by no stretch of the imagination a professional. Conversely, top level racing and rallying is an activity which is time-con-suming in the extreme, in which the period spent actually competing is the smallest part. The prep-aration and testing of cars, the reconnaissance of rally routes and making of pace notes, general administration and travelling to the competition venues, leaves little time for anything else. For the driver at the top of his particular tree, much of any otherwise unoccupied time will be taken up by personal appearances on behalf of his backers.

In any case, motor sport at the top level is such an expensive business that only a person of extensive private means can get there without outside assistance. Of those who have reached the top, none of whom the writer has heard in modern times has refused the fruits of his labours.

Similarly, virtually all motor sport is linked, to at least some extent, with the motor industry. Originally, this was the same industry as that which provides the sort of motor cars seen on the roads at any time of the day. More recently, a specialized motor sport industry has grown up, particularly in connection with circuit racing. This is now a substantial and virile industry but it retains close links with the big car makers and, even more, with the component manufacturers. Even so, the main industry continues to participate in motor sport and can be seen to reap many benefits from it.

Undoubtedly, the best example in modern times of a motor manufacturer taking an active interest in motor sport is the Ford Motor Company, mostly in Europe and especially in the UK. At one time, Ford participation was mainly as a willing supporter of those who used Ford cars and parts but, in the early 1950s, the participation became an involvement of increasing success and an energetic competitions department evolved. Initially Ford participated mainly in rallies but, with the advent of the Cortina, a racing programme was undertaken. The Cortina became the most successful competition car in the world and the Escort followed with even greater success.

Following a close association with them in the development of production engines for competition, Ford commissioned Cosworth Engineering of Northampton to build first a Formula 2 racing engine and then the V8 Ford DFV Formula 1 engine which has dominated Grand Prix racing for years and is the most successful Formula 1 unit in the history of motor racing. A parallel programme in the USA resulted in the GT40 winning the classic French Le Mans 24-hour race and America's own great classic, the Indianapolis 500 with a special V8 engine.

In comparison with the Ford efforts in both the UK and, more recently, in Germany as well, other European manufacturers have involved themselves in competitions on a smaller scale but quite effectively. At one time, constituent companies of what is now British Leyland were deeply involved in motor sport. The Mini-Cooper was the top competition car for several years, with innumerable racing and rally successes, Jaguar cars won at Le Mans consistently, Coventry Climax engines were the most successful in Formula 1 and Formula 2, and Austin-Healeys were among the most successful rally cars.

On a more limited scale, Chrysler and Vauxhall in Great Britain, Fiat, Lancia and Alfa Romeo in Italy, Citröen, Simca and Renault in France, Saab and Volvo in Sweden, Mercedes-Benz, Opel and Volkswagen in Germany, Toyota and Datsun in Japan, Holden in Australia and even Moskvich in Russia have embarked on competition programmes (mostly in the rally field) with considerable success. Some, of course, like Mercedes-Benz and Alfa Romeo, have honourable records in the highest levels of the sport in earlier days.

The components industry has been even more closely involved and many makers of tyres, fuel and oil, brakes and brake linings, shock absorbers, carburettors and fuel injection equipment, pistons and bearings, ignition and lighting equipment, etc., have been an essential part of the motor sporting scene ever since the very beginning, using races and rallying as a development ground for their products and as a means of earning publicity.

Motor sport is a great breeding-ground for publicity and so sponsorship has become an integral part of it. Originally it took the form of the provision of cars, petrol, oil, tyres and so on, usually with cash support. In recent years the scope has widened enormously to include any form of financial support which would result in reaping publicity. The original supporters remain, because they are essential to the whole operation but, in addition, we now have cigarette companies putting up very large sums to support teams – e.g., John Player, Philip Morris (Marlboro) and Embassy – with others, of which Rothmans-Carreras are the best example, sponsoring championships and individual race meetings.

Cosmetics are well represented, particularly by Yardley as consistent supporters of the McLaren team, to be followed by Wella for both race championship and team support.

Sponsorship has become an industry of its own, with small organizations acting as brokers, bringing together teams and drivers and sponsors. People have found sponsorship from a remarkably wide range of sources in industry, entertainment and other fields. It seems that if there is a company or person with money available for publicity purposes, it or he can be linked with motor sport in the form of sponsorship.

1 : HISTORY OF MOTOR SPORT

Motor sport is almost, but not quite, a 20th-century activity. Apart from early participation of steam-driven vehicles, and the occasional electric device, it is almost entirely a sport of the petrol-driven car, the intrusion of gas turbines, etc., being no more than spasmodic.

It is generally agreed that the first real motor competition was the Paris–Rouen Trial of 22 July 1894. To get the record strictly correct, there was a much earlier competition which the French publication *Vélocipède* tried to organize in 1887. However, since there was but one competitor (the Comte de Dion with one of his light steam cars, who did at least complete the distance in good form), this event near Paris scarcely qualifies for the normally accepted definition of a competition.

The Paris–Rouen Trial was announced by the magazine *Petit Journal* at the end of 1893 and was an enormous success from the very beginning. Indeed, by the closing date for entries there were no fewer than 102 'cars' due to take part. However, the majority were no more than figments in the imagination of their entrants. Besides the petrol- and steam-driven cars which, by then, were relatively common, and the entirely feasible electric vehicles which were, in fact, just beginning to appear, there were some highly unlikely means of propulsion listed. Among them were 'Automatic', gravity (also described as 'weight of passengers'), systems of pendulums and levers, hydraulic and some less extraordinary ones such as compressed air and gas. In the event, nothing using other than petrol or

17

steam propulsion appeared. There were 21 starters, and a few more that failed to pass preliminary trials, of which several followed the official runners along the route out of Paris.

Possibly because he was on record as having been the 'winner' of the only previously recorded competition, the Comte de Dion was flagged off first in the Paris–Rouen Trial of 1894. He was driving what we should describe today as a steam-powered articulated vehicle. It looked like a car towing a horse carriage with its front wheels removed. Amusing though that may sound in these days, it was not headed throughout the event.

The 1894 event was not a race, but the records show that de Dion reached Rouen first, about five minutes ahead of Lemaître's petrol-driven Peugeot $3\frac{1}{2}$ horsepower car, having averaged 11.6 mph for the $78\frac{3}{4}$-mile route. No fewer than 17 of the official starters completed the distance, Archdeacon's Serpollet steamer being the last to be clocked in after 13 hours running. By the standards of the time, this must have been an extraordinarily high proportion of finishers and amply justified the aims of the organizers to demonstrate the effectiveness of the mechanically-propelled vehicle, or 'horseless carriage'.

Awards were made on the basis of merit rather than performance and first prize was shared between Peugeot and Panhard-Levassor, whose cars made up the majority of the finishers. De Dion-Bouton was awarded second prize on the understanding that the steam car, requiring a mechanic to keep the engine going as well as a driver to control the vehicle, was not entirely within the spirit of the competition. It was the first, but by no means the last, discrimination against the steam car by motoring competition organizers.

Bearing in mind the long gap between the 1887

event of *Vélocipède* and the 1894 competition organized by the *Petit Journal*, the subsequent progress of motor sport was extremely rapid. Except during the periods of the two world wars, motor sport has an unbroken record of activity, although its intensity has fluctuated somewhat as a barometer of world prosperity.

There was to be no seven-year interval between the 1894 Paris–Rouen and the next motoring competition. The Comte de Dion and his friends lost no time in setting about the organization of a sequel. This time it was not just a short trial but a race in the form we understand today. It was immensely ambitious for its time, nothing less than a non-stop (so far as rivalry was concerned) event from Paris to Bordeaux and back again, a distance of 700 miles. It was to be the first of the great town-to-town races which were to be a feature of motor sport in the early years. The body of enthusiasts organizing the event was the first committee of what was to be called the Automobile Club de France, the most famous of the great national automobile clubs responsible for motor sport throughout the world.

One of the few rules of their first competition was that the cars had to carry more than two people. Consequently, the first entry to finish, Levassor's Panhard, was not the winner. Levassor drove single-handed for over 48 hours to average 15 mph for the journey, a feat of endurance which began a tradition maintained to this day by some of the top drivers in the toughest and longest rallies.

This first great European town-to-town race was in June 1895. In the autumn of that year motor sport reached America. James Gordon-Bennett, proprietor of the *New York Herald*, had been a spectator at the 1894 Paris–Rouen Trial, and both he and W. K. Vanderbilt, Jnr, were among the subscribers to the prize fund for the 1895 Paris–Bordeaux–Paris race, so that America was not without influential people with an interest in motor sport. However, it was the *Chicago Times-Herald* which was behind the first recorded American event. This turned out to be something like a combination of *Vélocipède's* Paris Trial of 1887 and the 1894 Paris–Rouen Trial combined. There were 100 entries, but only two cars were available for the first part of the competition, these being a car of the Benz type, driven by Muller, and a Duryea, which retired. There were four more petrol-driven cars and two electric vehicles for the main part of the competition some three weeks later, but only the Duryea and Muller's car finished the course.

In each subsequent year, the extent of motoring competition increased on both sides of the Atlantic. The Automobile Club of France's Paris–Marseilles–Paris race in 1896, over a distance of 1,062 miles, was even more ambitious and this time it was rationalized by having overnight stops with controls. It was won by Mayade's Panhard-Levassor, averaging 15.7 mph. The event, lasting over a period of 10 days, was considered an enormous success, attracting over 30 entries of which nearly half covered the full distance.

The significance of the Paris–Marseilles–Paris race, however, is that for the first time competing cars were divided into clearly defined classes, while serious elimination trials were conducted to select competitive representatives of the tricycle class to compete against the more powerful four-wheelers.

In contrast, the 1896 American race, the New York Cosmopolitan, attracted only seven runners among the usual spate of entries but only one, a Duryea, managed to finish.

There were also two races that year in the Bordeaux area, where enthusiasm had been engendered by the previous year's Paris–Bordeaux–Paris affair.

The newly formed A.C.F. already had a rival organization in opposition to it.

In 1897, motor racing started with an event on the French Riviera which consisted of racing over the winding mountainous roads from Marseilles to Nice. This was a three-day meeting and on the third day there was a hillclimb at La Turbie, an event which has survived to the present day.

Once again, steam cars were dominant and the three-day event was won by a De Dion steam brake, driven by the Comte de Chasseloup Laubat. It was followed home by a Peugeot and two Panhards, the second of which was driven by René de Knyff, who was already becoming prominent as one of the leading racing drivers of the period. There were several more races in France during 1897 and the first organized competition in Great Britain was held in May. It proved to be a most disappointing event with only six cars taking part, none of which finished the course.

As the 19th century came to its close the sport of the automobile progressed steadily, particularly in France, with the Marseilles to Nice races becoming annual events in the early part of the year, and other races taking place in various parts of the country.

One of these was the Course de Périgueux which, in 1898, goes on record as being the first motor racing event in which fatal accidents occurred. The unfortunates were the Marquis de Montaignac, driving a Landry et Beyroux, and his mechanic, both of whom died from injuries received when their car overturned into a field and fell on top of them. By this time, too, the Paris to Bordeaux race was becoming a classic and was won in 1898 by René de Knyff in a Panhard, at an average speed for the $356\frac{1}{2}$ miles of 22.1 mph.

Town-to-town racing was reaching the height of

its popularity and national capital to national capital races became popular, such as Paris to Amsterdam and back, a distance (over the route taken) of almost 900 miles.

To average over 20 miles per hour in the cars and on the roads of the time must be considered a remarkable achievement. The Paris–Amsterdam–Paris race occupied over 33 hours of driving during six days; this event was won by Charron in a Panhard at an average speed of 26.9 mph.

Then, as now, there was controversy over the fact that manufacturers were building special racing cars in events which were supposed to be developing the ordinary touring car for the benefit of the normal motorist, and there was a good deal of jealousy between those who enjoyed factory support and those who did not.

As well as the long-distance races there were many trials and hillclimbs and, towards the end of the century, record-breaking also became popular, partly with a view to proving the capabilities of the vehicle and partly from the sheer quest for speed. One of the first recorded record-breakers was the Comte de Chasseloup Laubat, who achieved 39.3 mph in an electric car called the Jeantaud in December 1898. The following month Camille Jenatzy averaged 41.4 mph and was beaten by the Comte with 43.7 mph. A few days later he increased the speed to 50 mph and followed it up in March with an incredible 57.6 mph before deciding to really have a go at this record-breaking business. Accordingly, Jenatzy built a cigar-shaped electric car ('Le Jamais Content') in which he averaged 65.75 mph in April 1899, a record which was to stand for three years.

The century ended with races from Nice to Castellane to Nice, Pau–Bayonne–Pau, Paris–Roubaix, Paris–Bordeaux, Paris–St Malo, Paris–Trouville,

Paris–Ostend, Paris–Boulogne and Bordeaux–Biarritz. Perhaps the most important of all was the Tour de France covering a distance of over 1,350 miles during a period of seven days with one rest day. The route was from Paris to Nancy in the east, down to Grenoble in the south, across to Périgueux in the south-west, and up to the Normandy coast via Nantes to Cabourg and back to Paris. This event was won by René de Knyff's Panhard at 30.2 mph after nearly 45 hours of driving. Jenatzy was the last finisher (in a Mors), taking 166 hours!

Gordon-Bennett Races

As motor sport progressed, more and more interest was being taken and the Gordon-Bennett series of races, sponsored by James Gordon-Bennett, proprietor of the *New York Herald*, became one of the more important international competitions. This was not a race between manufacturers but a race between the national automobile clubs. France chose a very strong team consisting of René de Knyff and Messieurs Charron and Girardot. The opposition consisted of one Benz from Germany, one American Winton and Jenatzy in a Bolide representing Belgium. There was organizational chaos and the German Benz was withdrawn while the Bolide and Winton retired in the very early stages and de Knyff's Panhard did not last the distance. However, Charron and Girardot both finished well and, although the event was not thought successful at the time, it gave a new impetus to international competition with the interesting qualifications that to represent a country the car had to be made entirely in that country.

Great Britain was not represented in the first Gordon-Bennett Trophy event but at that particular time the great 1,000 miles trial of the Automobile Club of Great Britain and Ireland (soon to be called the Royal Automobile Club) was taking place. The following year's Gordon-Bennett Trophy was no more promising, with a complete withdrawal by the German team and only one English car, a Napier driven by S. F. Edge, going to the start. Even this was disqualified from the Gordon-Bennett Trophy itself as it was found that the English tyres were unsuitable. Therefore, it was fitted with French tyres and was not eligible for the Gordon-Bennett Trophy. However, this event was run as part of the Paris–Bordeaux race which was a highly successful event, though not for Edge whose car retired in the early stages with clutch trouble.

The big event that year was the Paris to Berlin race which attracted a huge entry, of which no fewer than 47 cars finished; the winner was Fournier in a Mors at an average speed of 44 mph. There were two other main categories – light cars (won by Giraud, Panhard) and voiturettes won by Louis Renault in one of his own cars with another Renault second. Renault's performance was especially creditable as he was well ahead of Giraud's light car class-winning Panhard.

Circuit Racing

As well as the town-to-town races there were also circuit events although not as we understand them today. The early 20th-century circuit was perhaps 80 miles round with open roads and towns en route, but it took the cars past spectators several times, enabling them to follow the course of the race in a way which was not possible with town-to-town events.

Despite the emergence of circuit racing, the great town-to-town events were due to be expanded and the big one for 1902 was the Paris–Vienna race which incorporated the Gordon-Bennett Cup. Once again, the only challenger to the French was an English team consisting of Austin in a Wolseley

Typical of the monster cars of the turn of the Century, the 70 horsepower (12,000 cc) Mors led the 1903 Paris–Madrid at the time of its abandonment

and Edge in a Napier. None of the French team survived and, despite many problems, Edge reached the finish of the Gordon-Bennett section of the race at Innsbruck; thus, for the first time, France lost the Gordon-Bennett Cup.

The Paris–Vienna race itself was won, much to the consternation of many, not by one of the big racing cars but by Marcel Renault in one of his family Renault light cars with 60 horsepower engine and 650 kilogram weight. Renault finished in 15 hours 47¾ minutes at 38.9 mph, nearly 13 minutes ahead of Henri Farman in a 70 horsepower, 1,000 kilogram Panhard which won the heavy car category.

The year 1903 was a crucial one for motor racing, being the year of the great Paris–Madrid race which changed the whole course of the sport. It was also the year in which Great Britain came onto the motor racing map.

The Paris–Madrid was to have been the greatest race up to that time, but instead it proved to be the greatest disaster. By the time the cars had reached

Bordeaux there had been innumerable accidents and many fatalities so that the event was stopped by edict of the French Government, backed up shortly afterwards by the Spanish Government. It was estimated that the event was watched by as many as three million spectators and the almost total lack of control resulted in some of them walking into the path of several competitors who ran off the road as a result. When the event was stopped the lead was held by Gabriel, in a Mors, who had averaged 65.3 mph. Second was Louis Renault in the first of the light cars. He had averaged 62.3 mph but, even if the Government had not stopped the race, he would not have gone further as his brother Marcel had been one of those killed.

Quite apart from the spectator menace (to be repeated so many times over the next 70 years during which, perhaps surprisingly, open road racing managed to survive), the lack of control over the construction of cars had resulted in some absolutely fearsome monsters with huge engines in in-

Half the size of the Mors (p. 25), the 1903 Renault 30 horse-power was very little slower and much easier to drive

credibly flimsy chassis. They were made even more dangerous by the crude and vulnerable tyres of the time. These cars were capable of speeds well in excess of 80 mph and had minimal brakes. Therefore it was not surprising that accidents were both common in their occurrence and serious in their consequences.

Having won the 1902 Gordon-Bennett race, it fell upon Great Britain to stage the 1903 event, which was impossible on the English mainland as motor racing was not allowed on the public highway. Accordingly, the race was staged in Ireland. Even this required an Act of Parliament, but it was eventually passed and an eliminating trial was held on private property in the form of speed trials and a hillclimb.

The British all-Napier team took on three Mercedes from Germany, two Panhards and a Mors from France, and two Wintons and a Peerless from America. The race consisted of seven laps using two circuits near Dublin with one circuit of road common to both. The total racing distance was 327 miles. Jenatzy in a Mercedes emerged as the winner, averaging 49.2 mph, and was followed home by de Knyff in a Panhard for France with A. Firmin's Panhard third.

With the major city-to-city and capital-to-capital races out of favour, the 1904 races were over relatively short circuits. The Gordon-Bennett Trophy was the most prominent and was organized in Germany as a result of the Mercedes win of 1903. Germany was challenged by France, Austria, Belgium, Italy and Great Britain, and most of these countries held eliminating trials. The British used the Isle of Man, starting that island's remarkable history of motor sport.

The British team consisted of Girling and Jarrott in Wolseleys and Edge in a Napier, who finished

27

9th, 12th and 13th of the 19 entries. The event was won for France with a team led home by Théry in a Richard-Brasier.

At this time, Italy was beginning to take a profound interest in motor sport with successful cars built by the FIAT company. A number of Italian drivers were coming into prominence, notably Lancia, Florio, Nazzaro and Cagno.

In America, the Vanderbilt Cup attracted a fine international entry although many of the European cars had been bought by American enthusiasts and the winner was Heath in a 90 horsepower Panhard at 52.2 mph.

Because they were discontented with the fact that they were allowed only three cars in the Gordon-Bennett series, despite the fact that they could have fielded more than all the rest of the world put together, the French proposed for 1905 to incorporate the Gordon-Bennett Trophy race with a new event – the Grand Prix of the Automobile Club de France. Eventually, this did not happen and the Gordon-Bennett Trophy was held after the usual eliminating trials (again the British ones being held in the Isle of Man) and resulted in yet another French win, once more with Théry in a Richard-Brasier first.

Another significant event in 1905 was the first Tourist Trophy race, held in the Isle of Man, and originally organized as an event for ordinary touring cars. The first of these races attracted 58 entries of which 42 started. The event was governed by a fuel consumption formula allowing one gallon for every $22\frac{1}{2}$ miles. The winner, J. S. Napier on an Arrol-Johnston, still had over a gallon of his $9\frac{1}{4}$-gallon allowance at the end, having averaged a speed of nearly 34 mph.

The Grand Prix

For 1906, the Gordon-Bennett Trophy was out of favour and the year was noteworthy for the first Grand Prix, held over a 64-mile course at Le Mans, and for the Targa Florio, an event which has continued up to the present time on various circuits in Sicily, of which the first was 93 miles round and had a difference in altitude on the route of well over 1,000 feet. An extraordinarily difficult race, it was won by Cagno in an Itala at only 29.1 mph, this reflecting the fact that there were something like 1,000 corners to each lap.

The first French Grand Prix was an immense success. The 32 entries consisted mostly of French cars but with Italian and German opposition. It was a two-day event covering 12 laps and over 12 hours racing, and it was won by Szisz in a Renault averaging 63 mph.

In 1907, perhaps mainly as a result of the success of the French Grand Prix, the Germans decided to organize the Kaiserpreis over a 73-mile lap in the Taunus mountains. Despite tremendous efforts by the Germans the race was won by Nazzaro in a FIAT, with Hautvast in a Pipe second, and Opels third and fourth.

By 1908, even Russia was caught in the motor racing craze, organizing a 400-mile race over terrible roads from St Petersburg to Moscow; this was won by Henery in a Benz at 51.4 mph. The French Grand Prix went from strength to strength and the 1908 race, won by Lautenschlager in a Mercedes at 69 mph, attracted no fewer than 48 entries.

However, not for the last time, motor racing had outgrown its own strength and the burden of producing racing cars proved to be too much for many manufacturers with the result that there was no Grand Prix in 1909 or, in fact, before 1912. From 1909 to 1911, Grand Prix racing was in abeyance and circuit racing was confined to small cars (voiturettes), yet speeds were equal to those of the 'monsters' of previous years.

The 1912 formula was almost formule libre. The only restriction was that the body width had to be a maximum of 69 inches. There was also a 'small' class with 3-litre engine capacity limit and a minimum weight of 800 kilograms (1,763 pounds). The twin-overhead-camshaft Peugeot designed by Ernest Henry had an engine capacity of 'only' 7.6 litres (the comparable FIAT was 15 litres!) but the Peugeot had four valves per cylinder and was a highly efficient machine for its time. The FIATs ran into fuel-pipe problems and the Peugeot of Georges Boillot won from Wayner's repaired FIAT, with Dario Resta's 3-litre side-valve Sunbeam third. The Peugeot's specification – shaft drive, Rudge-Whitworth wire wheels and its general lay-out – set the trend for racing cars which was to last for the next 45 years.

For 1913 the Grand Prix formula was effectively a fuel consumption specification in that the fuel was limited to 20 litres for each 100 kilometres of racing (i.e. 14.2 miles per gallon). This limitation did not stop speeds increasing and Boillot's winning Peugeot averaged 72.2 mph.

The year 1914 was that of the big showdown between France and Germany, anticipating the world-wide conflagration about to commence. It was also the first year of a modern-type racing formula with a maximum engine capacity of $4\frac{1}{2}$ litres and a ban on supercharging or the use of alcohol fuels. The influence of the Henry Peugeot was to be seen in that all cars but one (an unsuccessful sleeve valve design) used overhead camshaft valve gear and a number also used 4-wheel brakes (although not the winning Mercedes), while there was much greater interest by manufacturers in

One of the most advanced cars of its time, the 1914 Peugeot 4½-litre was driven by the French hero Georges Boillot in the Grand Prix

Grand Prix racing than for some time, with the return of FIAT and participation by both Sunbeam and Vauxhall.

The major battle was between Mercedes and Peugeot, and the hero was Georges Boillot who drove a stupendous race in an attempt to keep ahead of Mercedes, but this was the more powerful team and Lautenschlager was the winner of this last great race before World War I.

During the first two years of the war, Peugeot, Mercedes, Delage and Sunbeam went across to America to clean up the races there but, with American involvement in the war, even that racing came to an end.

Inter-War Years

After the end of the catastrophic war, the British and French sporting authorities decided not to support racing in 1919 and 1920, and the only significant events were the Indianapolis 500 and the Targa Florio. In 1919, both of these races were won by Peugeot, but at Indianapolis a Ballot was second

The British motor racing industry did not produce another Grand Prix winner for more than 30 years after the 1923 Sunbeam

using an 8-cylinder twin overhead-camshaft engine designed by Ernest Henry of Peugeot fame. Big-time motor racing returned to Europe in 1921, preceded by a successful Indianapolis win by the American Frontenac from very strong European opposition (Ralph de Palma leading with a Ballot for 200 miles), while the American Duesenberg car made a successful invasion of France to win the Grand Prix.

The 2-litre Grand Prix formula starting in 1922 introduced a great era of competition between FIAT, Sunbeam, Mercedes, Alfa Romeo, Bugatti, Delage and Duesenberg. FIAT dominated at both the French and Italian Grands Prix with cars driven by Merzaro and Bordino. The 1922 FIAT was another trendsetter, its shape being typical of racing cars for many years after. In 1923, the German entries were banned from the French Grand Prix at Tours, but there was a great race between FIAT and Sunbeam, the British cars having an engine designed by the man who built the previous year's winning FIATs and it was Segrave who won the race. FIAT had their revenge at the Italian (European) Grand Prix with Salamano winning after Bordino retired. Bordino had led for the first half of the event although he was driving with a broken arm—from a practice accident—and his mechanic was changing gear. This was the first international win of importance by a supercharged car.

The same pattern carried on throughout 1924 with Alfa Romeo prominent with wins at Cremona (with Antonio Ascari driving) and in the French (also European) Grand Prix at Lyons, with Campari at the wheel. However, Segrave's Sunbeam won the Spanish Grand Prix to record the last major British success in this type of racing for more than 30 years.

As it was the final year of the 2-litre formula there were no new designs for 1925 but highly modified Delages came to the fore, winning the French and Spanish Grands Prix; other events were won by Alfa Romeo and Bugatti.

The formula was changed to $1\frac{1}{2}$ litres for 1926, but with the onset of the world-wide depression there was little support and only Bugattis were ready for the French Grand Prix and had an un-challenged 1-2-3 win. In subsequent races, attempts by Delage and Talbot were not any more successful and the Bugattis won again in the Span-ish (European) Grand Prix, and in the Italian

A classic design, Vittorio Jano's eight-cylinder Alfa Romeo P2 won the French Grand Prix first time out

Grand Prix. Delage won the British Grand Prix at Brooklands from the unprepared Talbot team, although Segrave's Talbot led initially. The $1\frac{1}{2}$-litre formula was not popular with either constructors or drivers, but continued into 1927 with the addition of FIAT to the existing teams; on no single occasion did all the leading contestants compete together. By this time the Delage had been developed properly and won every race to take the European championship. The formula was very expensive in that small engines were made to work extremely hard and, with the severe financial situation prevailing in Europe at the time, the formula was abandoned as a failure.

Formule Libre

The only genuine Grand Prix in 1928 was the Italian event at Monza, contested mostly by 1925 or enlarged 1927 cars; Chiron won in a Bugatti. There was a return to formule libre in an attempt to keep major racing going and the German Grand Prix, officially a sports car race, saw a win for Mercedes with 7-litre supercharged cars and Caracciola leading home a Mercedes 1-2-3 on the new Nürburgring; this was a 14-mile circuit built to relieve unemployment, and it must stand as one of Hitler's more meritorious achievements. The 1929 formula depended on weight and fuel consumption, and was taken seriously only by Bugatti whose exciting Type 35 car, one of the most admired Grand Prix models of all time, dominated with Williams and Chiron winning the French and Spanish Grands Prix.

Much the same formula was used again the following year, but only for the French and Belgian Grands Prix; again Bugattis were the winners.

There was rationalization of a sort for 1931 in that formule libre prevailed, but the races were subject to a 10-hour minimum. Some splendid cars were

One of the greatest racing cars of all time, the Type 35 Bugatti was dominant for several years

built by Bugatti, Alfa Romeo, and Maserati, and these manufacturers, with Mercedes, had a fair amount of success throughout this period which continued into 1932 and 1933, but with the race limit being 5 to 10 hours for 1932, and 500 kilometres distance in 1933.

Politics in Motor Racing

In an attempt to bring about rationalization and perhaps reduce speeds, because some of the 1931–33 cars were getting extremely fast (e.g. the type 54 Bugatti had a 5-litre straight-8 engine), the formula agreed for 1934 to 1937 was very simple, specifying only a 750 kilogram maximum weight without the driver, fuel, oil or tyres. The motor sport law-makers were now to realize that political considerations were to influence motor sport substantially for the very first time, with the German Government intent on gaining national prestige from motor racing. So it did not prove to be the speed-reducing formula they intended.

Alfa Romeo, Maserati and Bugatti all prepared new versions of existing models in reasonable confidence, using 3-litre engines. But, knowing of a massive government subsidy for successful designs, Mercedes-Benz came out with a most advanced W25 model with straight-eight 3.3-litre engine and all-independent suspension, while Auto-Union took over the Porsche Type C design with 4.4-litre 16-cylinder mid-rear engine (the driver in front) and all-independent suspension. The new formula succeeded only briefly in its attempt to bring down speeds. The early races, which were not contested by the Germans, demonstrated a minor reduction in performance. However, at the Eifel races in June, Manfred von Brauchitsch raised the lap record for the Nürburgring comfortably in a Mercedes, with the Auto-Union close behind; this new German dominance sounded the death knell for the existing models from France and Italy.

Apart from the French Grand Prix at Montlhéry (when Alfa Romeo had a 1-2-3 win after all the Germans dropped out), it was Mercedes or Auto-Union all the way, with little competition from the rest.

Never before had such professional teams taken to the track and the pace of development was tremendous. For 1935, Mercedes-Benz went up to 4 litres and Auto-Union to 5 litres. These teams dominated the races with the exception of the moment of glory for the legendary Tazio Nuvolari in the Alfa Romeo at the Nürburgring, when this little Italian's incredible ability humbled the Mercedes-Benz and Auto-Union teams on their home ground despite Nuvolari having lost several minutes (when a fuel replenishment pump broke down), dropping him from first to fifth place. A drive with superhuman skill and daring brought him back to second place but it was a burst tyre on the leading Mercedes of von Brauchitsch which finally gave Nuvolari victory.

For 1936, Alfa Romeo developed a V12 4-litre engine but the Mercedes went up to $4\frac{3}{4}$ litres and Auto-Union to 6 litres, with over 500 horsepower. Once the ex-motorcyclist Bernd Rosemeyer had adapted to the problems of driving the difficult Auto-Union, this marque was dominant from mid-season.

The same story applied to 1937 in that Mercedes and Auto-Union were nearly unbeatable (Mercedes now with a 5.6-litre engine) so that eventually Nuvolari gave up the unequal struggle and joined Auto-Union in mid-season. The British had their first view of these fantastic cars when both Mercedes and Auto-Union visited the Donington Grand Prix in October, and Rosemeyer won for Auto-Union after a titanic struggle with von Brauchitsch in the Mercedes.

For 1938 there was a new formula of 3-litres with supercharged engines or $4\frac{1}{2}$-litres unsupercharged; both the great German teams were well prepared with new cars. Auto-Union suffered a severe setback

The Mercedes-Benz W125 of 1937 was the most powerful single seater circuit racing car ever built

when Rosemeyer was killed in a record-breaking attempt during the winter, but Hans Stück was talked back into the team and then Nuvolari also signed. It was some time before the phenomenally able Italian mastered the technique of driving the rear-engined cars at full power.

Auto-Union had some difficulty in getting their new models right, but Mercedes went well from the very beginning of the season and had an exceptionally powerful driving team of von Brauchitsch, Hermann Lang, Rudolf Caracciola and Richard Seaman – the first British driver to find a place in one of the world's leading Grand Prix teams. This first season of the new formula was definitely a Mercedes-Benz year with Auto-Union winning only at Monza, where Nuvolari excelled before his home supporters, and again at Donington Park – a spectacle about which some senior British enthusiasts are still talking.

For 1939, Auto-Union were again competitive but won only at the French and Yugoslavian Grands Prix. For British enthusiasts, there was a terrible tragedy when Seaman was burned to death at the Belgian Grand Prix at Spa, but soon, like the rest of the world, there were other things to think about apart from motor sport.

After World War II

Not surprisingly, motor racing was slow in getting under way after World War II as many of the circuits had disappeared, the organizational system had largely fallen apart, the cars and the drivers had been dispersed and the world as a whole was still taking time to recover from six years of battle. Interestingly, it was Spain, for whom motor sport had ceased before anywhere else (as a result of the Spanish civil war), which came back first with a Grand Prix. This was in 1946, but for most of the traditional racing countries it was the following year or even 1948 before top-line motor racing was going ahead once more. When it did, the new Grand Prix formula was for cars up to 1½-litres supercharged and up to 4½-litres without superchargers. This represented a compromise between the voiturette formula of pre-war days and the Grand Prix formula itself. Almost without exception, the early races were contested by pre-war cars, many of which had been kept in safe conditions, although the German cars had been plundered and dispersed to various parts of the world.

This meant that the Italians reigned supreme, first with the Maserati and then, when the team decided to contest Grand Prix racing seriously once more, the Alfa Romeo Type 158, which was not only the quickest car of the time but usually fielded the best team of drivers.

As well as Formula 1 – the Grand Prix formula – a secondary division of Formula 2 was established and this was for cars with engines up to 2,000 cc unsupercharged.

The British scene was as slow to get going again as elsewhere although not through lack of enthusiasm. Despite severe petrol rationing there was competition of a sort in the form of sprints and

Both before and after World War II, the Alfa Romeo Type 158/9 dominated its class of motor racing

hillclimbs, and by 1947 there was major circuit racing once more, although not on the English mainland but at Jersey, in the Channel Islands, and in the Isle of Man.

Brooklands, the great centre of the United Kingdom in pre-war days, had been sold to the Vickers Aircraft Company and was no longer available for racing. Neither was Donington Park, and so British enthusiasts had to look elsewhere. Luckily, the countryside was littered with wartime aerodromes, most of them with perimeter tracks in good condition and frequently of a shape to provide interesting racing. The two major circuits of this type to be developed on a permanent basis were Goodwood and Silverstone, both of which staged major meetings in the autumn of 1948.

British Enthusiasm

Many other circuits started up all over the country and the enthusiasm for motor racing was enormous – much greater than in any other part of the world. However, the post-war period was a difficult one financially, and in an effort to overcome this problem a new form of racing was developed by impecunious enthusiasts who formed themselves into the Half-Litre Club and built their own formula car powered by 500 cc motorcycle engines. With one or two exceptions, these soon began to conform to an established pattern, of which the Cooper was the most successful with the engine mounted behind the driver and driving the back wheels by chain through a motorcycle gearbox. Other successful designs were the Kieft and the Revis, while the front-wheel-drive Emeryson was one of the few which did not conform to the regular pattern. Initially, the J.A.P. speedway engine was the most popular, to be replaced later by the more sophisticated Norton overhead camshaft unit from road racing motorcycles. Eventually, this 500 cc formula was taken up internationally (as Formula 3) but nowhere else did it achieve the popularity of the British events.

For reasons never adequately explained, but perhaps mainly because of the enthusiasm of the British and the wide variety of circuits and speed venues available to them, motor sport underwent a complete transformation in the 1950s, and it was the British who led the way. Nurtured by innumerable club race meetings on virtually every weekend from early spring until late autumn, the British began to undertake a complete domination of motor racing and motor sport generally; this situation was to last until similar enthusiasm became world-wide and the sport became international in a way which was never achieved in the days before World War II.

It introduced the era of the professional, of which there had been hints from the Mercedes-Benz and Auto-Union teams in Germany in the days before the war, and also to some extent among the Italians, but the numbers involved were tiny with the truly professional drivers little more than a handful. Much more normal were those who, while being paid to drive for teams, earned the bulk of their income from other sources or were of private means. Among the first of the true professionals was Stirling Moss, who began his motor racing career in 1948 and established a pattern to which the majority of modern drivers conform. He appointed a manager (Ken Gregory) who not only organized his activities, but looked after his publicity and added greatly to his income in gaining contracts to endorse products, make personal appearances and invest his income in diversified activities.

Others found that in making cars to provide themselves with suitable competitive machinery they could succeed best by building replicas for sale, and it was not long before a thorough-going British motor racing industry grew up with first Cooper and then Lotus, Lola, Brabham, McLaren and many others following suit. At the same time, in Italy, Maserati and Ferrari among others were very productive. Ready markets appeared, not only throughout Europe but in North and South America, Africa, Australasia and Asia. The entire world took to the sport of motor racing, not to mention rallying and all the other diversifications of motor sport.

Driver Cult

Although it was the immense expansion of the car racing industry itself which made possible the great amplification of the sporting scene, it was only to be expected that the interest would steadily change from the machinery to the men. In pre-war days it had been the cars which were discussed most, and the talk was of the battle between Mercedes and Auto-Union. In post-war years it was of Alfa Romeo and Ferrari, but in time the discussion centred on whether Moss could beat Hawthorn, and whether either was capable of challenging Fangio.

In addition to the various types of single-seater, there was equal interest in all other types of cars for competition purposes. The typical race meeting was not one or two events, but six or seven, with the main event for Formula 1 cars, perhaps with a sub-division for Formula 2, but also a Formula 3 race, a sports car race, a saloon car race and perhaps one or two handicaps.

In time, even greater variety developed, particularly in the United Kingdom, and later in other areas of activity. Frequently, these new formulae resulted from a wish to keep the cost of racing to a minimal level, while also hoping to provide a new and simple type of racing to encourage the development of new drivers. The most successful of these new single-seater formulae has undoubtedly been Formula Ford, but before that came Formula Junior (which in time was redeveloped into the most recent levels of Formula 3) and there has been Formula Vee, Formula Super Vee and many others of which quite a few have been purely national, such as Formule Bleue in France.

Other Forms of Motor Sport

Whereas most of the emphasis and the majority of the historical material was concerned with motor racing this was, of course, only a small part of the motor sporting activity from the very beginning – although easily the most highly publicized. So-called reliability trials, hillclimbs, etc., almost entirely on public roads, made up the majority of sport for the vast proportion of participants, of whom most were nothing like professionals but enthusiasts who enjoyed competition with their cars. Inevitably, motor sport acted as a barometer to the finances of the times, and expanded and contracted according to the amount of money which most people had available to indulge their sport.

If there was anything which a car was capable of doing, somebody would make a competition out of it or, if not a competition as such, a demonstration so that it became a practice to search out obstacles to overcome. Over the years people have been the first to climb Snowdon and Ben Nevis, or carry out a trial from Paris to Peking, to drive across the middle of Australia or the length and breadth of Africa, or drive overland from London to Sydney, or travel faster on land than any previous person.

Between the two world wars motor sport became organized on a world-wide basis under the AIACR (The International Association of Recognized

Automobile Clubs), the fore-runner of the current International Automobile Federation (FIA) under which the rules of racing and the various classes were agreed. The peak of achievement in motor sport has always been Grand Prix racing with the French Grand Prix (starting in 1906) being the original and the prototype of all others. Initially these races were on public roads closed for the occasion but, more and more, as time went by, held on courses specially constructed for motor racing. This made the competitions safer for both competitors and spectators, and the whole operation was financed by charging for public admission.

Whereas the French Grand Prix has moved from one course to another throughout its entire history, the Italian Grand Prix, which must be regarded as the next most significant from the historical point of view, has been held traditionally at Monza in Northern Italy, although the first race in 1921 was at Brescia. Although it was a very difficult time for the world as a whole, the period of the late 1920s was notable for the inauguration of many of the world's greater races. The Belgian Grand Prix at Spa began in 1925, but there was no further race in the series until 1930. The Tripoli Grand Prix in Italian North Africa also began in 1925 and continued, except for a two-year gap in 1931 and 1932, right up to the early war period of 1940. The Spanish Grand Prix began in 1923. The German Grand Prix started in 1926 (first of all at the Avus track at Berlin, but it mostly took place at the Nürburgring which was opened in 1927).

The Monaco Grand Prix was later in starting, the first race being in 1929, but the success of this event inspired other 'round the houses' of which the most durable has been the Grand Prix of Pau in Southern France. Many people regard the Monaco Grand Prix as the most exciting event in the Inter-

Racing through the streets of Monaco

national calendar, with the cars racing through the streets of the Principality and with the pits at the side of the yacht harbour in one of the most picturesque settings of a motor race anywhere in the world.

Sports Car Classics

Sports car racing can rightly claim even earlier antecedents than Grand Prix racing. This was because it was the obvious development of the earliest races in which cars were just cars without being racing, or sports cars, or anything else. One of the earliest events staged with the express purpose of improving the ordinary car, as bought by the man in the street, and now established as the earliest event with a relatively continuous history is the Royal Automobile Club's Tourist Trophy Race.

Although a race, the TT began also as a sort of fuel economy run in that competitors were limited in the amount of fuel available to them and this was used as a check on outright performance. The allowance was $9\frac{1}{4}$ gallons for the four laps of the circuit totalling $208\frac{1}{2}$ miles, or $22\frac{1}{2}$ miles per gallon maximum consumption. There were 42 starters and the winner was J. S. Napier in an Arrol-Johnston whose average speed was 33.9 miles per hour. He managed to conserve petrol well enough to still have over one gallon left in his tank at the end of the race. A shorter course was held the following year when the four laps amounted to 161 miles. This time the petrol allowed was $6\frac{1}{2}$ gallons and the winner was the Hon. Charles Rolls, in a Rolls Royce, who averaged 39.29 mph and had barely a pint left in his tank at the finish. In time, the organizers dropped the consumption formula and other qualifications were used on the TT to define the eligibility for a race.

The Targa Florio was another island race, being held on the island of Sicily off the toe of Italy. It has always been one of the most difficult races in the calendar and has been held with greater consistency than most. The course has varied from the long Madonie circuit, of about 92 miles, to an entire lap of the island – approximately 600 miles – and there have been medium Madonie (67 miles) and short Madonie circuits, the latter being the most commonly used, with a lap of 44.6 miles. Even this has well over 100 major corners and many times more changes of direction.

For the Targo Florio there have been no high-minded ideals of improving cars for the common man, but a straightforward intention of providing the ultimate test for the sports cars and drivers of the time.

In contrast, the 24-hour race at Le Mans has tended to be one of the faster races and, as far back as 1953, the race average exceeded 100 mph. This has always been one of the longest races in the calendar and, for some parts of its history, it has been the most publicized race of the period.

Accordingly, it has received greater attention from manufacturers than have most other races and, in particular, Bentley, Jaguar and Ford all built cars specifically for this event, although they were also successful at other venues. The first 24-hour race at Le Mans was in 1923 and, although this is the same area as the original Grand Prix of 1906, it has never been the same circuit. The length of the track for the 24-hour race has varied between 10.7 and 8.3 miles. Le Mans was the scene of the worst-ever motor racing accident when, in 1955, over 80 people died as a result of a car crashing and being launched into the crowd opposite the pits. This had a profound effect on motor racing the world over. For instance, there has been no motor racing in Switzerland since that time.

Hillclimbs

The main motor sport activity in Switzerland since that period has been hillclimbing which, in a mountainous country, has considerable potential. From the earliest days, hills presented a challenge to the motorist and in the early competitions it was an achievement purely to complete the course. Once this had been achieved, the object was to complete the climb as quickly as possible against the stopwatch. This became a universal activity with such events as the Mont Ventoux hillclimb in France, the Trento-Bondone in Italy, the Freiburg in Germany, together with events such as Pike's Peak in America and Shelsley Walsh in England with their own very close following. There are highly organized competitions in most parts of the world, and three or four seasonal championships most years in England. But the main competition is the European Mountain Championship.

The very early reliability trials, designed to demonstrate to an unconvinced public that the motor car was an efficient form of transport and a real alternative to the horse and the steam train, developed in time into the rally. The various forms of test were to examine the ability of the driver and the capability of the car.

Among the supreme tests of the car has been record-breaking. In many ways this is the simplest form of motoring competition, yet it is one demanding the utmost performance. Record-breaking has always gone in phases and the peak of activity was in the years between the wars when the outright record, commonly known as the Land Speed Record, was raised from under 200 to nearly 400 miles per hour with Sir Henry Segrave, Sir Malcolm Campbell, George Eyston, John Cobb and the American Ray Keech among the more notable record-breakers.

Sir Malcolm's son, Donald Campbell, was also deeply involved with record-breaking in the Sixties, with a further 'Bluebird', but although he passed Cobb's 394 mph speed which had stood since 1947 as the 'car' record (a vehicle transmitting the power through its wheels) and exceeded 400 mph, by that time numerous Americans had gone half as fast again with devices more like wingless aircraft. These used straightforward 'jet' or rocket power which made the achievements of the conventional 'car' exponents seem relatively tame.

2 : THE DEVELOPMENT OF THE COMPETITION CAR

Except for Formule Libre, which is something of a rarity, all types of motor sport are distinguished by being restricted to a particular type of car.

The earliest competitions were purely for automobiles because the number of available competitors was insufficient to permit any divisions into types. Yet it was as early as 1896 when the first evidence of classes appeared and, in the Paris–Nantes–Paris race of September 1896, there were two classes for cars, with seats for up to and over four people, and two for motorcycles, those with and without pedals. There was also an additional class for any vehicle which didn't come into any of those categories.

The early town-to-town races tended to be divided into cars and light cars, with a possible additional division for three-wheelers and/or motorcycles. At the time there was nothing like a racing car, although it became an increasingly common practice for manufacturers to build special machines for competing in the races concerned. However, after a race it was normal for these vehicles to be sold and, perhaps fitted with more suitable bodywork, to pass into private ownership as touring vehicles for everyday use.

A considerable amount of jealousy occurred between competitors when some had the benefit of the latest works machinery and others did not but, almost invariably, the attitude had to be 'if you can't beat 'em, join 'em'. The single-seater racing car as such did not appear for many more years, partly

49

because for some time it was obligatory to carry a riding mechanic. Even after the mechanic was no longer required or was even banned from racing, the two-seater type body tended to prevail, because it was normal by that time to seat the driver low down on one side of the propeller shaft housing, which left an equal space on the other side of the shaft.

In time, the various types of cars evolved into single-seaters, sports cars and eventually saloons. There have, of course, been many variations on these themes.

The earliest cars were exceptionally diverse in character as might have been expected from an entirely new industry. They tended to have chassis consisting of beams of wood, often reinforced by steel plates, and on these beams were mounted the semi-elliptic springs which provided the suspension. The steering was by tiller and the drive was usually by chain to the rear wheels; it was already known from steam vehicle practice that a differential gear was necessary. An alternative to the wooden-beam chassis was the frame of hollow steel tubes which followed cycle practice of the time.

There was no set pattern for the position of the engine which might be in front or under the main seat. These early cars had rear-wheel braking only and were virtually platforms with seats attached. In 1896 cars were still using solid rubber tyres or even iron tyres although pneumatics had been produced. However, from then on, pneumatic tyres were regarded as an absolute necessity. It was at this period that people started building cars specially for racing and the expense of the sport began to make itself apparent. At this time, a car with an 8 horse-power rated engine was regarded as being very big and might weigh as much as 1,000 kilograms.

By the end of the century, tiller-steering had

given way to the steering-wheel and the familiar pattern of the car was for the engine to be in front, preceded by the radiator, the drive to the rear wheels being by chain after the gear mechanism. The engine, usually of four cylinders, was normally enclosed by a bonnet; the seats were at the rear and high up, and were of the bucket type, often with the passenger's seat slightly behind that of the driver.

After the early days, in which the rear wheels were much larger than the front ones, it was becoming more common by the turn of the century for the wheels to be of the same size at the front and rear. Very frequently the wheels featured detachable rims and the practice occurred of having spare rims with tyres already fitted. It was much quicker, of course, to fit these than repair the tyre in the event of a puncture. By the beginning of the 20th century the racing car was developing as a quite separate device from the touring vehicle. The Mercedes in which Werner won the Nice–Salon–Nice race in 1901 was rated at 35 horsepower and weighed just over 1,000 kilograms, but the Mors which won the Paris to Bordeaux race later the same year was a 60 horsepower model weighing 1,300 kilograms. The 1,000-kilogram upper weight limit of 1902 did not prevent Panhard from building a 70 horsepower model and in the fatal Paris to Madrid race of 1903, which was stopped at Bordeaux, there were Mercedes cars of 90 horsepower and Gobron-Brillié cars rated at 110 horsepower. It was notable, however, that the Renault which was the first car to reach Bordeaux and which was placed second in general classification, was rated at a mere 30 horsepower and was within the 650-kilogram limit for the light car class. At 62.3 miles per hour it was only 3 mph slower than the leading 70 horsepower Mors of Gabriel.

The 60 horsepower Mercedes of 1903 was a trendsetting car in that it used a pressed steel frame and this feature was adopted also by Panhard and Mors in the same year. With speeds reaching over 70 mph, attempts were being made at streamlining the cars, but this conflicted with the requirement of keeping the engine cool by means of a large radiator. The best way to achieve this was to mount the radiator at the front, which defeated any serious streamlining techniques.

By 1904, 'heavy' cars (which meant the genuine racers) were more often than not of 90 or 100 horsepower, and weight saving was being achieved by extensive lightening of the chassis by drilling holes, etc.; it was also becoming common to use fairly light materials for the bodywork. One hundred and forty horsepower cars were common by 1905. They had more efficient transmissions which resulted in the abandonment of chains in favour of shaft drive, and the cars became much more closely identifiable with those used today.

The adoption of accepted formulae brought about rationalization to the layout and a great deal of ingenuity was used by engineers to extract more power from their engines, with enormous benefit to the passenger cars of subsequent years. While the single-seater racing car pioneered the new developments, these were taken up rapidly for sports cars, which were the prototypes of the touring vehicles of the day. The frequent efforts by legislators to retain some semblance of normality in the designs resulted in a rapid rub-off of technical achievement into the road-going cars of the period. In particular, tyres, brakes, and lubricants all benefited enormously from competition, and events such as the 24-hour race at Le Mans did much to improve headlights, hood design, etc.

Racing Cars

From being just a car designed for the single purpose of going more quickly than its rivals round a track or along a road, the racing car has developed steadily during three-quarters of a century to become a device of incredibly specialized form, using aerodynamics as well as mechanical engineering and extreme forms of advanced tyre technology to achieve its ends.

The development into a single-seater, which was finalized in the late 1920s, produced a general pattern which, on the whole, did not alter significantly for nearly another 30 years. The accepted outline specification was for a slim car (if possible, not much wider than a man's hips) conforming to the expected format of nearly all other cars – a radiator ahead of an engine, a gearbox behind the engine, driving a rear axle by means of a propeller shaft. Mostly, the driver would sit over the shaft but, occasionally, it passed alongside him, allowing him to be positioned much lower. Models based on this overall design were made with slight variations to the form of front or rear suspension, the type of springing, the system of brake operation, the number of cylinders or their size, and the shape of the bodywork.

Occasionally, there were experiments to break away from this pattern, of which the Auto-Union P-Wagen of the middle and late 1930s was the most notable example. This put the engine behind the driver, who sat much nearer the nose of the car. The gearbox was next to the engine and drove straight into the rear wheels.

Like many of the designs of Dr Ferdinand Porsche, it was years ahead of its time. Undoubtedly it would have been a world-beater but for the excellence of its contemporary, the Mercedes-Benz W125. This, a car of 'conventional' design, was

One of the most exciting racing cars ever was the Auto-Union P-Wagen, shown 'in flight' at Donington Park

mostly superior. Although immensely powerful, it was less difficult to control than the Auto-Union. It is possible that, with continued development, the Auto-Union's inherent problems would have been overcome, but World War II intervened.

The immediate post-war cars were mostly predictable developments of the pre-war designs, but the desire to produce a genuinely low-cost formula in Great Britain resulted in the 500 cc single-seater, with a single-cylinder motorcycle engine behind the driver, turning the back wheels by means of a chain. From this crude beginning, the modern racing car developed steadily. The Cooper was the most successful of the early 500s and this make also developed in due course to the first successful Formula 2 ($1\frac{1}{2}$-litre) and Formula 1 ($2\frac{1}{2}$-litre) designs with the engine behind the driver.

These Coopers broke the hitherto largely unquestioned supremacy of the front-engined racing car and brought about a revolution in single-seater design of such completeness that, today, the mid/rear engine car is accepted as the norm. The first Cooper success with a rear-engined Grand Prix car was in 1958. By 1961, there was no serious contender with any other layout. Since that time, the development has become highly sophisticated.

Early fears that the 3-litre formula introduced in 1966 would cause serious traction problems, owing to a surplus of power, have proved unfounded. This is because of enormous strides in suspension and tyre technology, which have made it possible to harness outputs of close to 500 horsepower (very much more in other forms of racing, notably the North American Can-Am sports cars), aided by aerodynamics to ensure that the wheels stay firmly pressed down onto the track surfaces.

'Wings' on racing cars work the opposite way round to that in aircraft, pushing the machine down into closer contact with the road. Their first use was seen in the Chaparral sports car of 1967 and Ferrari introduced them into Grand Prix racing in the middle of the following season. Within weeks, every other constructor was using them. Their efficiency in achieving their purpose, resulting in greatly improved wheel adhesion and therefore higher cornering speeds, was undisputed. However, lack of knowledge on their application resulted in a number of serious incidents, a prime example occurring when both Lotus cars of Graham Hill and Jochen Rindt suffered 'wing' support breakages, causing major accidents on the same corner of the Spanish Grand Prix. Restrictive legislation

The Cooper-Climax changed the face of motor racing and ended the success run of front-engined Grand Prix cars

'Wings' at their most ridiculous—the Brabham of Piers Courage at the Spanish Grand Prix

controlling the use of these aerodynamic devices resulted.

Development along the lines of the Cooper design theme led to near-standardization of the Grand Prix car, with most other forms of racing car following suit in due course. Great Britain became the home of the Formula 1 car (with the notable exception of Ferrari of Italy), based in the southern half of England.

This trend was encouraged by the ready availability of proprietary engines and gearboxes from British manufacturers. First were the Coventry Climax units (developed initially from fire pump engines) in the $2\frac{1}{2}$-litre formula of the late 1950s and the V8 $1\frac{1}{2}$-litre of the first half of the sixties. These were followed by the 3-litre Ford Cosworth DFV which became available to constructors from 1968 and is the most successful racing car engine of all time. The Hewland gearbox became equally obvious as a choice of transmission.

For almost the entire history of the sport, the prime mover of the racing car has been the conventional four-stroke petrol-burning piston engine, although the steam engine was a serious contender in the early days. Equally, power has been put through the rear wheels with few exceptions. Thus the racing car has reflected the normal layout of the passenger car for most of the time. Major divergencies have been the use of the supercharger to force into the cylinders more fuel/air mixture than atmospheric pressure is able to do, the use of exotic fuels instead of petrol (mostly alcohol but also, in post-war years, highly explosive oxygen-bearing fuels such as nitro-methane), the employment of the diesel engine (notably in the Indianapolis 500) and the gas turbine.

Racing cars accelerated the acceptance of four-wheel brakes in contrast to the early cars which had brakes on the rear wheels only. For a time, during which it was thought that the rear wheels alone could not cope with the output of a modern Grand Prix engine, experiments were made with four-wheel-drive. So far, nobody has managed to produce a four-wheel-drive system which, in the end, proved more efficient (in terms of the ultimate test – lap times) than the time-honoured two-wheel-drive system, but four-wheel drive has many theoretical attractions.

However, the development cost has proved to be enormous and most of the incentive has been taken away by the continued ability of modern racing tyres to transmit all the power available onto the road. Over 1,000 horsepower has been spoken of in connection with turbo-charged Can-Am sports cars.

Sports Cars

The sports car has been developed alongside the racing car, sharing its advances and, very occasionally, having something to offer as an improvement which racing car designers have been pleased to adopt. Two examples which come to mind are the disc brake and aerodynamic downthrust aids. The disc brake, already appreciated in the aircraft industry, gave Jaguar sports cars an enormous advantage in the Le Mans 24-hour race. It was soon to be seen on British Formula 1 cars, before gaining world-wild acceptance not only in motor racing but, in time, for all types of passenger car.

The Chaparral sports car's use of an inverted 'wing' to apply downthrust has already been mentioned and this brought about an even more rapid reaction from racing car constructors. Interestingly, Chaparral demonstrated a 'ground effect' system in a subsequent season, extracting air from under the car to keep it more firmly in contact with the road (i.e., the hovercraft principle in reverse) but this development, and the complexity it threatened, resulted in an outright ban by the authorities governing motor racing in North America.

When the sports car developed as a separate class of vehicle is difficult to define. Initially, the typical road-going car was, of necessity, a type of sports car, because only sporting-minded people were interested in cars. The family saloon was much later in coming along, although occasional examples of elegant closed coachwork were to be seen from the earliest times.

As the racing car progressed towards the single-seater, the idea of the sports car emerged as a high performance vehicle for use on the road, giving near racing performance but with accommodation for at least one passenger alongside the driver. Eventually, regulations were drawn up to ensure that sports cars in competition complied with minimal requirements to guarantee their usefulness for normal everyday motoring. Long-distance races such as the Tourist Trophy and the Le Mans 24-hour Grand Prix d'Endurance were the typical racing events which identified sports cars.

British manufacturers thrived on the type, with

Bentley, Alvis, Lea-Francis, Riley, Singer, MG as just a few of the many famous names involved. The Italians had Alfa Romeos, the French their Bugattis, although sometimes there was not much difference between the sports two-seaters and the Grand Prix cars of these two.

Bearing in mind that the cars required wide bodywork to enclose two seats, sports cars were a long time in making serious use of streamlining to increase their performance by reduction of drag. It was not until the 1950s that extensive use was made of wind tunnels to exploit the outline shape of the car's bodywork to this end.

Inevitably, some constructors interpreted rules their own way to gain advantages and this led to more complex regulations for defining cars more carefully. Today, the regulations which govern sports cars (and all other types of car, for that matter) are so detailed that there are few loopholes and the dimensions of bodywork, seats, their positioning, etc., are controlled precisely.

This has not meant, however, that the racing sports car has developed along the lines of a car for the road and although, in recent years, provision has been made to maintain the space which could be occupied by a passenger, that has been just about the only concession. In effect, sports cars have become two-seater racing cars, of even greater complexity than the single-seaters with which they have frequently shared the majority of their mechanical parts. In consequence, they have become even more expensive than the single-seater racing car.

The ultimate sports car has been the Can-Am (Canadian–American Challenge series) machine, definitely the fastest and most powerful track or road-going device yet made. With engines of 8-litres or so capacity, some using turbo-charging to provide even more performance, they have reached outputs of over 1,000 brake horsepower, or more than double those found in Grand Prix or Formula 5000 single-seaters.

Yet, by means of this evolution, the sports racing car has helped to develop a large number of highly enjoyable road sports cars, which have given their owners a standard of performance and roadholding far in advance of that available in most other types of road-going car of the time, albeit with mostly lower levels of amenity.

Grand Touring Cars

A near relation to the sports car, possibly its successor, is the GT car (GT = Grand Touring or Gran Turismo). The typical early GT car was a sports two-seater with handsome closed bodywork, providing more comfort and better luggage accommodation than the sports model from which it was derived. It was literally a car in which to go touring in a grand manner, cruising at high speed across the continents in days when speed limits did not occur outside towns.

In time, as the sports racing car became less and less like anything which could be used for road transport, the GT car came into its own right as the sporting car for the road. In its turn, it had races organized for it and, although competition-minded constructors did the obvious thing in building special racing versions which came within the rules but did without the comforts, it went on to become possibly the most enjoyable form of road car available to the enthusiastic driver.

Saloon Cars

The saloon car did not figure seriously as a motor sporting machine until fairly recent years. Except when special coachwork was placed on what otherwise would have been a sports car (e.g. a few early

Bentleys were given saloon bodywork which did not seriously mar their performance), the majority of saloons of past years have been heavy, unwieldy and relatively low-powered. In consequence, they were largely unsuited to sporting activities, apart from participation in reliability trials.

The situation changed in post-war years, however, as the motor sporting scene expanded, rallies became world-wide and saloons became faster and more roadworthy. Rallying and racing went hand in hand in their development of the sporting saloon and most car manufacturers have used motor sport both as a platform for publicity and a means of achieving rapid improvements for their vehicles.

Most car-making firms have developed competition departments in conjunction with component and tyre manufacturers, and with the encouragement and active participation of oil companies. Working in close co-operation with their design and service divisions, these departments have been able to improve their companies' products, find out quickly what broke and how to prevent such breakages, make the vehicle faster and more reliable, and win prestige for their companies.

Saloon cars in competition have provided immense amounts of information which has been used to make the basic product far better. Performance, handling and reliability have all benefited, and a special breed of high performance saloon (often called a 'GT' model) has been developed for the competitions field, while providing customers with a much more enjoyable type of car at a cost not much greater than that of the normal model.

Events such as the Monte Carlo Rally have improved winter motoring amenities, the World Cup and Safari rallies have produced tougher suspensions and transmissions, and innumerable production saloon races have reaped untold benefits in brakes, tyres and so on. Among cars affected are Minis, Ford Zephyrs and Jaguar Mark VIIs in England, Opel Kadetts and Simca 1000s in Europe, and Chevrolets, Fords and various Chryslers in North America, with Holdens, other Fords and Chryslers in Australia, not to mention South American Volkswagens and Russian Moskvichs.

Eventually, it was realized that the mass-produced saloon body can be both light and very rigid, and an ideal basis on which to build a car for racing and rallying. The result has been some extremely rapid and roadworthy cars of relatively low cost, such as the Mini-Cooper S, the Ford Escort RS 1600, the Chevrolet Camaro, the Simca Rallye 1000, the Opel Commodore GS/E and the Datsun Violet 160J SSS.

Just as in the earliest days of motoring, if you've got a car, you can put it into competition.

Production saloon car racing—Hillman Avenger GT

3 : GRAND PRIX FORMULAE

1906: Minimum weight 1,000 kilograms (2,204 lb).

1907: Fuel limited to 30 litres per 100 kilometres (9.4 miles per gallon).

1908: Maximum piston area 755 sq. cm (117 square inches). Minimum weight 1,150 kilograms (2,534 lb).

1912: Maximum width of car 175 centimetres (69 inches).

1913: Fuel limited to 20 litres per 100 kilometres (14.2 miles per gallon) – the fuel had to be carried in a standard style 'bolster' tank at the rear. Minimum weight, without fuel, 800 kilograms (1,760 lb). Maximum weight 1,100 kilograms (2,425 lb).

1914: Maximum engine capacity 4.5 litres. Superchargers and alcohol fuels banned. Weight limits as in 1913.

1922–1924: Maximum engine capacity 2.0 litres. Minimum weight empty 650 kilograms (1,433 lb).
Up to this time, two persons in a car, minimum weight 120 kilograms (264 lb) or ballast to this amount.

1925: Maximum capacity 2.0 litres. Minimum weight empty 650 kilograms (1,433 lb). Two-seater body (minimum width 80 centimetres –

31.5 inches) but driver only carried from now on.

1926: Maximum engine capacity 1.5 litres. Minimum weight 600 kilograms (1,322 lb). Two-seater bodywork, minimum width 80 centimetres (31.5 inches).

1927: Maximum engine capacity 1.5 litres. Minimum weight 700 kilograms (1,543 lb). Single or two-seater body, but minimum width 85 centimetres (33.5 inches).

1928: Minimum weight 550 kilograms (1,212 lb). Maximum 750 kilograms (1,653 lb). Minimum distance 600 kilometres (373 miles).

1929: Minimum weight 900 kilograms (1,980 lb). Minimum body width 100 centimetres (39.3 inches). Pump fuel. Maximum consumption of fuel and oil 14 kilograms per 100 kilometres (20 litres liquid measurement or 14.2 miles per gallon).

1930: As for 1929, but with the addition of 30 per cent benzole permitted.

1931: Formule Libre with a minimum race duration of 10 hours.

1932: As for 1931 but race duration between 5 and 10 hours.

1933: As for 1931/2 but race distance 500 kilometres.

1934–1937: Maximum weight 750 kilograms (1,653 lb). Minimum body width 85 centimetres (33.5 inches). The weight was for the car including oil and four wheels but without water, fuel, tyres, tools, spare parts or spare wheel.

1938 and 1939: Maximum engine capacity 3.0 litres supercharged or 5 litres unsupercharged. Minimum weight 850 kilograms (1,873 lb). The weight was without water, fuel, wheels or tyres, oil or tools, spare parts, etc.

1946–1953: Up to 1.5 litres supercharged or 4.5 litres unsupercharged. (After 1951 very few races were run to this formula and the majority of events in 1952 and 1953 were organized to the then-current Formula 2– up to 2.0 litres unsupercharged.)

1954–1960: Up to 2.5 litres unsupercharged (also up to 750 cc supercharged – although there were no serious entrants at this capacity limit). From 1954 to 1957 inclusive, there was no fuel restriction. 1958–60 carried the same capacity limits, but there was now a fuel limitation in that petrol had to be used, this being of the aviation spirit type at this period.

1961–1965: Over 1,300 cc and up to 1,500 cc unsupercharged, running on pump petrol. Minimum weight 450 kilograms (991 lb).

1966–probably until end of 1979: Up to 3.0 litres unsupercharged or up to 1.5 litres supercharged. Maximum number of cylinders 12. Minimum weight 575 kilograms (1,268 lb). Running on pump petrol.

4 : CURRENT RACING CAR FORMULAE

Except for purely national or local events, motor sport throughout the world is organized for cars complying with formulae or specifications laid down by the international controlling body which is the Sporting Commission of The International Automobile Federation. There are many divisions of which the highest is the Grand Prix formula, and each is defined clearly to avoid confusion and to ease the task of those who have the responsibility for controlling the sport and ensuring fair play.

Formula 1   Formula 1 is the Grand Prix formula and the present specification was due to have expired on 31 December 1975 (having started on 1 January 1966), but it is likely to continue until December 1979. There is provision for gas turbine engines and this type of propulsion has in fact been used in world championship and other Formula 1 races, notably in the form of the Lotus 56B with Pratt and Whitney engine. Generally the formula is for engines with reciprocating pistons and with a capacity of up to 3,000 cc without a supercharger, or 1,500 cc with a supercharger, and a maximum of 12 cylinders. There is a minimum weight of 575 kilograms (1,268 lb) and there are various controls over body width, fuel tanks, oil storage tanks and a requirement for cars to carry a fire extinguishing system. The type of structure which a car shall have is laid down so that in the event of an accident the driver shall be substantially protected from the effects of the crash. There is a limit on the amount

The Formula 1 Hesketh is typical of modern Grand Prix cars, powered by the Ford Cosworth DFV engine

of petrol which can be carried; this must not exceed 250 litres (55 Imperial gallons), and not more than 80 litres may be carried in any one tank. Generally speaking, in all major competitions sanctioned by controlling bodies in most parts of the world, the fuel used must be petrol as available in pumps and similar to that sold to the public.

Formula 2   Formula 2 is for single-seater racing cars with piston engines not more than 2,000 cc unsupercharged. There is a minimum weight of 500 kilograms (1,102.5 lb). Up to 1 January 1976, the engine must be derived from a series production engine recognized by the FIA as being produced at the rate of at least 1,000 units per year. Extensive modifications are permitted but the engine block and cylinder head must be identifiable as from an internationally recognized car. There is a limit of five forward gears in the gearbox, and the drive must go through only two wheels of the car. As from 1 January 1976 until 31 December 1977, when the formula is due to be replaced, the origin of the engine will be free, but not more than 6 cylinders will be permitted. Safety measures with regard to crushable structure of the car are as for Formula 1.

Formula 3   Formula 3 is for single-seater racing cars and is intended to be the training ground for drivers to gain experience before Formula 2 and Formula 1. There is a maximum cylinder capacity of 2,000 cc with not more than 4 cylinders. Engines, particularly the block and cylinder castings, must be those of an internationally recognized car of which there is a series production of at least 5,000 units per year. The other most important requirement is that the induction to the engine must be through a throttling flange of 24 millimetres maximum diameter. Air going into the engine has to pass through this hole. There are dimensional requirements of a minimum wheelbase of 200 centimetres (79 inches), a minimum track of 120 centimetres (47 inches), and a maximum wheelrim width of 25.4 centimetres (10 inches). In addition, there is a maximum tyre tread width restriction of 20 centimetres (8 inches), and a minimum weight limit of 440 kilograms (970 lb).

The most successful Formula 2 car of the Seventies has been the March, with BMW engine

Stepping stone to greater things, Formula 3 can lead to Grand Prix success. Tom Pryce winning the F3 race at Monaco, 1974

There are some general requirements for all the Formulae 1, 2, and 3: the vehicles must be weighted in running order with all lubricants and cooling liquids carried, but without fuel. They must be equipped with a reverse gear and an automatic starter with electrical or other source of energy carried aboard the car (although in Formula 1 or Formula 2 it is permissible for cars on a dummy grid to be started with the help of a supplementary battery). The driver's seat and the car construction must be such that the driver has an easy exit, which must not take more than 5 seconds. The cars must be equipped with a six-point safety harness, i.e. with two shoulder straps, abdominal straps and two crutch straps. The wearing of the safety harness is obligatory. Each of these types of car must have a dual-circuit braking system, an oil catch tank to collect any oil spilling out of the engine or transmission, and may not be replenished with oil during a race. All three types are required to have safety

Rivalling Formula 1 for maximum power, Formula 5000 cars are possibly even more demanding to drive

fuel tanks designed to avoid rupturing and therefore spilling fuel in an accident.

Formula 5000 This formula started as Formula A in North America and was adopted in the United Kingdom as Formula 5000 and in Australasia as the Tasman Formula. The title of Formula 5000 has now become universal. The title '5000' refers to the engine capacity and almost without exception the cars use North American type V8 5,000 cc engines with the Chevrolet being the only one considered successful. The Tasman Series Repco engine is also based on the same General Motors unit. Officially, the engine capacity is from a minimum of 2,750 cc up to a maximum of 5,000 cc and the engines must be derived from those recognized internationally under Groups 1 or 2, i.e. with a minimum production of either 5,000 or 1,000 units per year. In engines up to 3,500 cc, all Group 2 modifications and any homologated options (for example, 4-valve cylinder heads etc.) are permissible, but those engines over 3,500 cc must be of a type only using two push-rod operated valves for each cylinder and the cylinder heads themselves must be of standard type.

There are minimum weight limits of 550 kilograms (1,225 lb) for cars up to 3,500 cc and 612 kilograms (1,350 lb) for 3,501–5,000 cc cars. All the safety requirements applicable to Formula 1 also apply to Formula 5000.

Formula Atlantic Formula Atlantic is, as the name implies, applicable to both North America (where it originated as Formula B) and Europe, although the regulations governing the machinery differ slightly on each side of the ocean. The European version includes the Ford BDA engine which is not acceptable in North America. This formula is for single-seater racing cars with an engine capacity over 1,100 cc but not exceeding 1,600 cc. Supercharging is not permitted. There is a minimum weight limit of 440 kilograms (968 lb). Fuel injection systems are permitted except on the Ford BDA engine, but this unit is almost universal in Great Britain. There is a maximum of five forward speeds permitted in the transmission and a maximum fuel tank capacity of 15 gallons. There are strict limits on the modifications which are permitted but the Ford BDA engine, which is used so widely, is capable of producing around 200 horsepower in its Formula Atlantic form. As well as this engine there is a range of Alfa Romeo, BMW, Datsun, Fiat, Ford Push-Rod, Ford Twin-Cam, Porsche, and Renault 1,600 engines but, to date, none except Ford engines have been used successfully. The general requirements of the formula are similar to those in Formula 2.

USAC-Indianapolis Formula The North American oval-track formula is administered by the United States Automobile Club and the Indianapolis 500-mile race is the main event. This is for single-seater racing cars with racing engines of

The most successful low-cost racing car formula of all time, Formula Ford has produced many leading drivers

up to 2.65 litres supercharged or up to 4.2 litres un-supercharged or up to $5\frac{1}{4}$ litres if of non-over-head-camshaft production origins. There is also provision for gas-turbine engines, but these and refinements such as four-wheel-drive have been effectively outlawed by restrictive regulations.

Formula Ford   This was initially a purely British formula developed from racing school training cars at Brands Hatch; it has now become international and, with variations, is to be found in Australia, Africa and North America as well as in Europe. The basic single-seater car conforms roughly with Formula 3 requirements and there is a minimum weight limit of 400 kilograms (882 lb) but there are major differences of which the most important are that the engine is restricted to the standard push-rod over-head valve Escort Sport 1.6-litre engine, and road wheels must be used. Aerofoils and other aero-dynamic devices are banned, the chassis must be of tubular rather than of monocoque construction, the gearbox must not have more than four forward speeds and the car must use rear-wheel-drive only;

torque biasing or limited slip differentials are not permitted. From 1975, a single type of Dunlop racing tyre is obligatory for British races.

Formula Vee   This is another international single-seater formula to encourage new drivers. It is based on the 1,300 cc Volkswagen and engine tuning is limited very strictly, although outputs of perhaps 95 horsepower are possible. As well as the use of the 1,300 cc Volkswagen engine and gearbox, the suspension units and wheels must also be from the Volkswagen Beetle car, but racing tyres are used. Formula Vee is contested throughout Europe and also in North and South America.

Formula Super Vee   This is a much more sophisticated formula and the 1,600 cc Volkswagen engine is used with a greater degree of tuning permitted, while the chassis and running gear of the car is not restricted. The engine output is reputed to be in the region of 145 horsepower and this, with the other freedom from restriction, results in much faster racing than with Formula Vee. There are greatly increased costs, but greater rewards.

Formule Bleue   This is a French national single-seater formula based on Citroën GS mechanical parts with an engine of 1,015 cc. It is supported financially by Total and Michelin.

Formule Renault   This is a French national formula using the Gordini Renault 1.6-litre engine.

Formula 4   A British national classification for rear-engined single-seater racing cars. The engine must be of British manufacture, either Ford, British Leyland or Chrysler, with a maximum capacity of 1,000 cc, a single carburettor choke only may be used and there is a restrictor with an internal diameter not exceeding 36 millimetres. Only four forward gears are allowed, and torque biasing, locked or limited slip differentials are banned.

Monoposto Formula   Another entirely British single-seater formula for cars with construction by their owners or proprietary built cars constructed prior to 30 September 1968. Aerodynamic devices are forbidden and the engines must have push-rod operated valves only and be of production type with a maximum capacity of 1,600 cc.

Clubman's Sports Cars   Open-wheeled sports cars of a British national formula type with set dimensions as to bodywork, etc. These must use British Ford or British Leyland push-rod overhead valve engines with not more than four-speed gearboxes, but there are no restrictions on engine tune generally, except for one sub-division. There are two classes – Class A: 1,001–1,600 cc fully tuned. Class B: Engines up to 1,600 cc in Formula Ford state of tune.

Group 5 Sports Cars   These are the internationally recognized two-seater competition cars built especially for racing on closed circuits. Apart from having to comply with general dimensional specifications, for body width, seat size, etc., these cars bear few restrictions. When taking part in the World Championship for Makes (i.e. the World Sports Car Championship) there is an upper capacity limit of 3,000 cc and the cars run concurrently with Special Grand Touring cars (see opposite). There is also a Group 4/Group 5 European Championship for makes with an upper limit of 2,000 cc.

Clubman's sports cars are a special British creation combining low cost with high speed

Group 4 Special Grand Touring Cars These are a form of limited production car with at least two seat accommodation and which have been built in numbers of not less than 500 units within a 24-month period.

Group 3 Production Grand Touring Cars These have at least two seats and a production of at least 1,000 units within a 12-month period. Modifications permitted are very limited (i.e. no more than for Group 1 saloons – see page 76).

Successful Group 5 sports car of the mid-seventies, the Alfa Romeo T33

Developed from road cars, but with extreme bodywork modifications and 'full race' engines, the Group 4 Special GT racing Porsche 911

Can-Am Sports Cars   These cars comply with international Group 7 and the Sports Car Club of America's sports racing category. They are nominally two-seater full-width body sports cars with a minimum engine capacity of 2,500 cc and no maximum capacity limitation. These are the fastest competition cars on the track that the world has yet seen, with supercharged engines of up to 8 litres capacity and power outputs in the region of 1,100 horsepower.

Group 1 Saloons   Production saloon car racing has assumed great popularity in the past few seasons and these are intended to be cars nearly identical with those bought by the general public. To be eligible, the cars must be made in numbers of not fewer than 5,000 identical models within a 12-month period. Modifications permitted are confined mainly to safety requirements, such as roll-over cages being fitted inside the cars, but substantial improvements in performance may be gained by the process known as 'blue-printing', whereby engines are carefully rebuilt using ideally matched parts so that a near-perfect specification can be

Closely related to standard road cars, Group 1 saloons (like this Triumph Dolomite Sprint) are allowed a certain amount of modification

achieved. In British events there are two levels of production saloon car racing. National events are divided by engine capacity classes and the cars may use racing tyres. At club racing level, the divisions are by price and road tyres must be used. Variations in regulations in various parts of the world can result in substantial differences in performance.

Group 2 Saloon Cars These are officially 'Special Touring Cars' and are either Group 1 cars subjected to considerably more modification, or cars with a minimum production of 1,000 units within 12 months. As with Group 1 cars, these must be four-seaters unless their engine capacity is no more than 700 cc. Substantial improvements may be produced by modifying standard parts, substituting larger valves, etc., modifying the engine induction system, fitting different exhaust systems, cam-shafts, valve gear, etc. Group 2 Saloon cars are frequently matched against Group 3 Production Grand Touring cars and tend to be faster, especially when the latter are confined to modifications similar to those which are permitted in Group 1.

Special Saloons This is the free-for-all club saloon car formula which allows any modification providing the outline shape of the car is unchanged. It is not uncommon for completely different types of engine to be fitted, e.g. Ford BDA engines in Minis, the Formula 1 Ford V8 in Escorts and Capris. Consequently, very high performances result.

Super Saloons (or Superloons) This branch is an upward extension of special saloons, mainly for those of very high performance usually with large engines installed in small, very light bodywork. General outline similar to production saloons.

Modified Sports Cars This category replaces the earlier Marque classification and is for two-seater sports cars of production type, but permitted to have substantial modification providing the same type of engine is used as in the original. Bodywork has to continue looking like that of the standard car.

Production Sports Cars (Prodsports) These are Group 3 Production Grand Touring Cars limited to the modifications which are similar to those allowed for Group 1 Saloons. While the general types of car are often similar to those seen in Modsports races, the much restricted tuning which is permitted results in substantially less performance. Unlike most other forms of competition, production sports cars race according to price categories rather than engine capacity classes.

Sports GT Cars These comply with any of Group 3 or 4, 5 or 7 of the International Sporting Code and are basically two-seater sports racing cars.

Formule Libre   This is quite literally 'free formula' – in other words no restrictions whatever. Today it can be used as a basis for making special regulations for a particular type of competition, but more objectively it is to provide a completely open race without any restrictions, with the possible exception of the requirement to run on pump petrol. Formule libre races are used frequently in various underdeveloped parts of the world where there are insufficient cars to make up a race under any of the recognized classifications. More often (and especially in British club racing), it is used to provide fast and relatively spectacular racing by mixing together all types of single-seater and sports cars. In recent years, the one important formule libre race was the Rothmans 50,000 at Brands Hatch of 1972, the 50,000 indicating a prize fund of £50,000. More usually, however, such races are at relatively unimportant meetings with token prizes – i.e., the winner gets a slightly larger cup than the second man.

5 : CLASSIC RACING CARS

1903 Mors (France) Huge four-cylinder (11,559 cc) 70 horsepower racing car with mechanically-operated inlet valves and chain drive transmission. Capable of about 85 mph. Leader of Paris–Madrid race (driven by Gabriel) when it was abandoned at Bordeaux. It is possibly the peak achievement of a company which was in racing from 1897.

1903 Renault (France) When the Paris–Madrid race was abandoned, this 'light car', driven by Louis Renault, was second, with only the huge Mors quicker, yet its four-cylinder engine was 'only' 6.3-litres, rated at 30 horsepower. Used shaft drive (as all Renaults) and mechanically-operated inlet valves.

1914 Mercedes (Germany) Winner of the final great pre-war Grand Prix (Lautenschlager), this 4.5-litre developed 110 horsepower, with four cylinders, an overhead camshaft and dual ignition by magnetos. First Mercedes racer to use shaft drive but still had rear wheel brakes only. Top speed about 100 mph. Also won 1915 Indianapolis 500.

1914 Peugeot (France) Vanquished in French Grand Prix, this car survived to win 1916 Indianapolis 500 (second to Mercedes in 1915) and various other victories. Most advanced car of its time, with 112 horsepower from 4.5 litres, with twin-overhead camshafts and four valves per cylinder, shaft drive and four-wheel brakes.

1923 Sunbeam (Great Britain) Product of Anglo-French Sunbeam-Talbot-Darracq combine

Successful on both sides of the Atlantic in 1914/15, the 4½-litre Grand Prix Mercedes was very modern in design

and a near-replica of 1922 FIAT. A six-cylinder 2-litre with twin-overhead camshafts and roller-bearing crankshaft. Segrave's French Grand Prix win at 75.3 mph the last formula GP win by a British car for 32 years.

1924 Alfa Romeo P2 (Italy) Vittorio Jano's classic 2-litre eight-cylinder with 2 ohc, roller bearings, supercharger and 134 horsepower output. Career began with first-time-out win of French Grand Prix (Campari) in period of intense competition. Design revived in 1930 as sports car for Targa Florio win (Varzi).

1924 Bugatti Type 35 (France) Produced in 1½-, 2- and 2.3-litre forms for several years in both supercharged and unsupercharged versions, this is one of the all-time greats, winning the Targa Florio in four successive years and innumerable other races. Notable for cast aluminium wheels and superb workmanship.

1928 Bentley 4½-litre (Great Britain) Nicknamed by Bugatti 'the fastest truck', this four-cylinder car was developed directly from the 1922 3-litre. The 1928 Le Mans victory was second in series of four 24-hour race wins (3-litre in 1927, 6.5-litre in 1929 and 1930). Car very similar to customer models.

1931 Alfa Romeo 8C-2300 (Italy) Another Jano design with eight cylinders, 2 ohc and supercharger. Standard sports car developed 142 horsepower, but up to 180 horsepower was produced later. Won at Le Mans (Howe/Birkin) and Targa Florio (Nuvolari) in first season, while racing car version won Italian Grand Prix (Campari/Nuvolari).

1935 ERA B-type (Great Britain) Using engine based on Riley production unit with pushrod ohv, this was intended mainly for 'Voiturette' (1½-litre) racing, but also built in 1,100 cc and 2-litre form. Initiated by same group as later BRM, it won innumerable races before and after the war.

1936 Auto-Union P-Wagen (Germany) Most successful year of the first competitive rear-engined racing car. Supercharged V16 with 520 horsepower from 6.1 litres. Difficult handling from swing rear axles overcome by Rosemeyer's driving to win European championship, with victories over Mercedes-Benz at Eifel, German, Swiss and Italian Grand Prix.

1937 Mercedes-Benz W125 (Germany) Final version of the most powerful single-seater circuit racing cars ever built, with supercharged V12 5.7-litres and 646 horsepower, running in the 750-kilo-

(left) The 1928 Bentley 4½-litre sports car at Le Mans

(centre) The versatile Alfa Romeo 8C-2300 of circa 1931

(bottom) The simple ERA was successful for many years after 1935

gram formula intended to limit power output! Wishbone front suspension and de Dion rear axle provided better handling than rival Auto-Unions.

1937 BMW 328 (Germany) Production sports car with advanced six-cylinder pushrod ohv engine. Output up to 130 horsepower resulted in domination of 2-litre sports car races and 1940 Mille Miglia win. Post-war copy of engine design by Bristol used successfully in Bristol, Frazer-Nash and AC sports cars and F2 Cooper.

Alfa Romeo 158/9 (Italy) Dominant from 1938 to 1951, the 'Alfetta' had a straight-eight engine with 2 ohc. Outputs rose from 190 horsepower initially to nearly 400 horsepower, with modifications, including increased supercharger boost. Early cars had all-independent suspension but final model had de Dion rear axle.

1952/3 Ferrari 500/F2 (Italy) Seldom has a Grand Prix car dominated so completely as this four-cylinder 2-litre. For the 1952 and 1953 seasons, the world championship was for Formula 2 cars and this won 14 out of the 15 races, i.e., all but the 1953 Italian Grand Prix, won by Fangio's Maserati.

1954/5 Mercedes-Benz W196 (Germany) Revolutionary in design, the W196 was almost unbeatable (aided by the best drivers of the era – Fangio and Moss). It was a space-frame chassis with fuel-injected eight-cylinder engine having desmodromic valve gear, all-independent suspension (low pivot swing rear axles) and inboard brakes.

1954 Maserati 250F (Italy) Competitive during the free-fuel period of the $2\frac{1}{2}$-litre formula, the 250F helped Fangio to world championships in 1954 and again in 1957. Good handling car with

(right) The
BMW 328
sports car was
very advanced
for its time

(above)
complex but
reliable, the
Mercedes-Benz
W196 of
1954/5

(right) Almost
unbeatable—
the Ferrari
500/F2 of
1952/3

simple space frame, six-cylinder engine, wishbone front suspension and a de Dion rear. Developed steadily to include fuel injection.

1955 Jaguar D (Great Britain)   Successful elsewhere but built primarily for Le Mans, where it won first in 1955, the year of spectator disaster. Won also in 1956 and again in 1957, when five cars ran, finishing 1-2-3-4 and 6. Monocoque body/chassis with six-cylinder 2 ohc engine of 3 to 3.8 litres.

1957 Vanwall (Great Britain)   Initiator of British dominance in Grand Prix racing, starting with win in 1957 British Grand Prix, followed by 1958 manufacturers' championship. Four-cylinder 2 ohc engine with Bosch fuel injection, in Colin Chapman space-frame chassis with strut rear suspension, disc brakes and Frank Costin aerodynamic bodywork.

1959 Cooper-Climax (Great Britain)   World Championship winning car of 1959 (and again, in revised form, 1960), resulted in revolution of Formula 1 design and, eventually, most other racing cars, with engine behind driver. Four-cylinder Coventry Climax FPF 2 ohc engine. Direct development of single-cylinder 500 cc F3 cars.

1962 Lotus 25 (Great Britain)   First monocoque Grand Prix car, narrowly missing 1962 World Championship and winning easily (seven GP wins for Jim Clark – an all-time record) in 1963, when Coventry Climax FWMV V8 $1\frac{1}{2}$-litre engine had fuel injection. Pattern for most subsequent Grand Prix cars.

1966 Ford GT40 (Great Britain/USA)   Aimed at Le Mans success and developed from 1963 Lola GT, this car failed at first two attempts (but won elsewhere). In 1966, had a 1-2-3 win. Mark IV

(above) One of the last of the successful front-engined GP cars, the Maserati 250F

(centre) Jaguar D-type—closely related to road-going sports Jaguars

(bottom) Lotus Climax 25, fore-runner of most modern GP cars

model won again in 1967 and Gulf-Mirage versions also won next two years' races.

1967 Lotus 49 (Great Britain) Built around Ford Cosworth DFV 3-litre V8 engine used as part of main chassis structure, carrying rear suspension. Won first time out (Clark, Dutch Grand Prix). Gave Graham Hill World Championship, 1968. In 1970, Rindt gave the '49' its third successive victory at Monaco Grand Prix.

1970 Lotus 72 (Great Britain) Most successful Grand Prix car since start of World Championship. Victories 1970 to 1974 inclusive, providing championships for Rindt (1970) and Fittipaldi (1972) and total of 20 GP wins. Features include wedge shape, variable rate suspension, inboard front brakes, side radiators and Ford Cosworth DFV engine.

The most successful Grand Prix car ever is the Lotus Ford 72 (John Player Special)

6: CLASSIC RACES

French Grand Prix

More correctly called the Grand Prix of the Automobile Club de France, this is the original Grand
Prix from which all others take the name. It has
been held at more than a dozen different venues
since it began and over twenty different circuits
have been used. For instance, the track at Le Mans
where the first race was held in 1906 bore no relation
to that section of the modern 24-hour race circuit
which was employed for the 1967 Grand Prix.

After more than fifty races, it is possibly invidious
to choose any particular events as more outstanding
than the rest, but the 1914 duel at Lyons between
the French hero Georges Boillot and the Mercedes
team, who were eventually victorious; the 1953
Rheims side-by-side battle between the veteran
Juan Manuel Fangio in a Maserati and the relative
newcomer Mike Hawthorn in a Ferrari, won by the
latter; together with the surprise victory (also at
Rheims, in 1961) of the Italian Giancarlo Baghetti
(Ferrari) in his very first world championship
Grand Prix, must all go down in motor racing history as exceptional.

French Grand Prix results

			Speed mph/kmh
1906	(Le Mans)	Szisz (Renault)	62.88/101.19
1907	(Dieppe)	Nazzaro (Fiat)	70.61/113.64
1908	(Dieppe)	Lautenschlager (Mercedes)	69.05/111.13
1912	(Dieppe)	Boillot (Peugeot)	68.51/110.26
1913	(Amiens)	Boillot (Peugeot)	72.12/116.07
1914	(Lyons)	Lautenschlager (Mercedes)	65.57/105.52
1921	(Le Mans)	Murphy (Duesenberg)	78.10/125.70
1922	(Strasbourg)	Nazzaro (Fiat)	79.33/127.71
1923	(Tours)	Segrave (Sunbeam)	75.35/121.27
1924	(Lyons)	Campari (Alfa Romeo)	70.97/114.21

			Speed
			mph/kmh
1925	(Montlhéry)	Benoist/Divo (Delage)	69.72/112.21
1926	(Miramas)	Goux (Bugatti)	68.12/109.69
1927	(Montlhéry)	Benoist (Delage)	78.12/125.72
1928	(Comminges)	Williams (Bugatti)	84.86/136.57
1929	(Le Mans)	Williams (Bugatti)	82.64/133.03
1930	(Pau)	Etancelin (Bugatti)	90.38/145.45
1931	(Montlhéry)	Chiron/Varzi (Bugatti)	78.22/125.88
1932	(Rheims)	Nuvolari (Alfa Romeo)	92.32/148.57
1933	(Montlhéry)	Campari (Maserati)	81.49/131.14
1934	(Montlhéry)	Chiron (Alfa Romeo)	85.05/136.88
1935	(Montlhéry)	Caracciola (Mercedes-Benz)	77.40/124.57
1936	(Montlhéry)	Wimille/Sommer (Bugatti)	77.85/125.28
1937	(Montlhéry)	Chiron (Talbot)	82.48/132.73
1938	(Rheims)	Von Brauchitsch (Mercedes-Benz)	101.13/162.76
1939	(Rheims)	Muller (Auto-Union)	105.25/169.38
1947	(Lyons)	Chiron (Talbot)	78.09/125.66
1948	(Rheims)	Wimille (Alfa Romeo)	102.96/165.69
1949	(Rheims)	Chiron (Talbot)	99.66/160.87
1950	(Rheims)	Fangio (Alfa Romeo)	101.84/168.72
1951	(Rheims)	Fangio/Fagioli (Alfa Romeo)	110.97/178.59
1952	(Rouen)	Ascari (Ferrari)	80.13/128.96
1953	(Rheims)	Hawthorn (Ferrari)	113.65/182.88
1954	(Rheims)	Fangio (Mercedes-Benz)	115.68/186.18
1956	(Rheims)	Collins (Ferrari)	122.29/196.80
1957	(Rouen)	Fangio (Maserati)	100.02/160.96
1958	(Rheims)	Hawthorn (Ferrari)	125.46/201.89
1959	(Rheims)	Brooks (Ferrari)	127.44/205.08
1960	(Rheims)	Brabham (Cooper)	131.92/212.31
1961	(Rheims)	Baghetti (Ferrari)	119.84/192.87
1962	(Rouen)	Gurney (Porsche)	101.84/163.89
1963	(Rheims)	Clark (Lotus)	125.31/201.67
1964	(Rouen)	Gurney (Brabham)	108.77/175.04
1965	(Clermont-Ferrand)	Clark (Lotus)	89.22/143.58
1966	(Rheims)	Brabham (Brabham)	136.89/220.32
1967	(Le Mans)	Brabham (Brabham)	98.89/159.16
1968	(Rouen)	Ickx (Ferrari)	100.44/161.64
1969	(Clermont-Ferrand)	Stewart (Matra)	97.91/157.25
1970	(Clermont-Ferrand)	Rindt (Lotus)	98.42/158.39
1971	(Paul Ricard)	Stewart (Tyrrell)	111.66/179.70
1972	(Clermont-Ferrand)	Stewart (Tyrrell)	101.56/163.45
1973	(Paul Ricard)	Peterson (John Player Special)	115.12/185.26
1974	(Dijon)	Peterson (John Player Special)	119.76/192.73
1975	(Paul Ricard)	Lauda (Ferrari)	116.63/187.65

Italian Grand Prix

Next to the French Grand Prix, the Italian race in the world championship series is the most venerable. With few exceptions it has been held at Monza, one of the fastest of the world's Grand Prix circuits, with or without the banked section which nearly doubled the length of the track. This combined 'road' and banked track, which is very unpopular with competitors, was used in 1955/56 and 1960/61.

Even without the banked section, the average speed exceeded 150 mph (241 kmh) in 1971 and subsequently the track has been slowed by the addition of chicanes on the quickest sections, as had been done for similar reasons from 1934 to 1948. Despite this, the Italian round of the championship still produces heart-stoppingly close racing at great speed, usually with slip-streaming bunches of cars. Normally the final race of the Grand Prix season in Europe, Monza frequently produces the year's champion, amid scenes of great excitement.

Italian Grand Prix results (at Monza unless indicated otherwise):

			Speed mph/kmh
1921	(Brescia)	Goux (Ballot)	89.94/144.74
1922		Bordino (Fiat)	86.90/139.85
1923		Salamano (Fiat)	91.03/146.50
1924		Ascari (Alfa Romeo)	98.74/158.90
1925		Brilli-Peri (Alfa Romeo)	94.82/152.60
1926		'Sabipa' (Bugatti)	85.87/138.20
1927		Benoist (Delage)	90.05/144.93
1928		Chiron (Bugatti)	99.36/159.90
1930		Varzi (Maserati)	93.48/150.44
1931		Campari/Nuvolari (Alfa Romeo)	96.79/155.78
1932		Nuvolari (Alfa Romeo)	104.09/167.52
1933		Fagioli (Alfa Romeo)	108.58/174.74
1934		Fagioli/Caracciola (Mercedes-Benz)	65.36/105.18
1935		Stück (Auto-Union)	85.18/137.08
1936		Rosemeyer (Auto-Union)	84.10/135.35
1937	(Leghorn)	Caracciola (Mercedes-Benz)	81.59/131.30

		Speed *mph/kmh*
1938	Nuvolari (Auto-Union)	96.77/155.73
1947	Trossi (Alfa Romeo)	70.33/113.19
1948	Wimille (Alfa Romeo)	70.37/113.26
1949	Ascari (Ferrari)	105.04/169.04
1950	Farina (Alfa Romeo)	109.69/176.54
1951	Ascari (Ferrari)	115.52/185.92
1952	Ascari (Ferrari)	110.04/177.09
1953	Fangio (Maserati)	110.68/178.13
1954	Fangio (Mercedes-Benz)	111.98/180.21
1955	Fangio (Mercedes-Benz)	128.49/206.79
1956	Moss (Maserati)	129.74/208.79
1957	Moss (Vanwall)	120.27/193.56
1958	Brooks (Vanwall)	121.21/195.08
1959	Moss (Cooper)	124.39/200.18
1960	P. Hill (Ferrari)	132.06/212.53
1961	P. Hill (Ferrari)	130.11/209.39
1962	G. Hill (BRM)	123.62/198.94
1963	Clark (Lotus)	127.74/205.57
1964	Surtees (Ferrari)	127.77/205.63
1965	Stewart (BRM)	130.46/209.96
1966	Scarfiotti (Ferrari)	135.92/218.75
1967	Surtees (Honda)	140.50/226.12
1968	Hulme (McLaren)	145.41/234.02
1969	Stewart (Matra)	146.97/236.52
1970	Regazzoni (Ferrari)	147.08/236.70
1971	Gethin (BRM)	150.75/242.61
1972	Fittipaldi (John Player Special)	131.61/211.81
1973	Peterson (John Player Special)	132.63/213.45
1974	Peterson (John Player Special)	135.41/217.90

Belgian Grand Prix

The character of the Belgian Grand Prix has changed drastically in the seventies, owing to the decision not to use the magnificent but frighteningly fast Spa-Francorchamps circuit where, in 1970, the 3-litre cars were lapping at well over 150 mph (241 kmh). Not only has this circuit immensely quick corners, but also a reputation for sudden changes of weather in the late spring, when the Belgian race is held, so that one part of the circuit can be dry and the other awash.

Such conditions have resulted in serious accidents when cars have reached the wet area for the first time. In any case, many drivers feel that the Spa course, consisting largely of public roads, is basically unsafe by current GP standards. Others greatly regret the passing of one of the most challenging circuits in the GP calendar, which undoubtedly sorted 'the men from the boys'. Perhaps there is too much emphasis in people's memories on the fatal accidents which have occurred in the Belgian Grand Prix and not enough is recalled of the great feats of driving which have provided so much excitement.

Belgian Grand Prix results (at Spa-Francorchamps unless indicated otherwise):

			Speed mph/kmh
1925		Ascari (Alfa Romeo)	74.36/119.67
1930		Chiron (Bugatti)	72.10/116.03
1931		Williams/Conelli (Bugatti)	82.01/131.98
1933		Nuvolari (Maserati)	89.23/143.60
1934		Dreyfus (Bugatti)	86.91/139.97
1935		Caracciola (Mercedes-Benz)	97.87/157.50
1937		Hasse (Auto-Union)	104.07/167.50
1939		Lang (Mercedes-Benz)	94.39/151.90
1946	(Brussels)	Chaboud (Delahaye)	67.07/107.94
1947		Wimille (Alfa Romeo)	95.28/153.43
1949		Rosier (Talbot-Darracq)	96.95/156.02
1950		Fangio (Alfa Romeo)	110.05/177.10
1951		Farina (Alfa Romeo)	114.26/183.88
1952		Ascari (Ferrari)	103.13/165.97
1953		Ascari (Ferrari)	112.47/178.00
1954		Fangio (Maserati)	115.08/185.20
1955		Fangio (Mercedes-Benz)	118.84/191.25
1956		Collins (Ferrari)	118.43/190.59
1958		Brooks (Vanwall)	129.93/209.10
1960		Brabham (Cooper)	133.62/215.03
1961		P. Hill (Ferrari)	128.15/205.23
1962		Clark (Lotus)	131.89/212.25
1963		Clark (Lotus)	114.10/183.62
1964		Clark (Lotus)	132.79/231.40
1965		Clark (Lotus)	117.16/188.56
1966		Surtees (Ferrari)	113.94/183.36
1967		Gurney (Eagle)	145.98/234.93
1968		McLaren (McLaren)	147.14/236.79
1970		Rodriguez (BRM)	149.95/241.31

				Speed mph/kmh
1972	(Nivelles)	Fittipaldi (John Player Special)		113.35/182.41
1973	(Zolder)	Stewart (Tyrrell)		107.74/173.38
1974	(Nivelles)	Fittipaldi (Texaco-Marlboro)		113.11/182.03
1975	(Zolder)	Lauda (Ferrari)		107.06/172.28

Monaco Grand Prix

Sole survivor among the world championship events of the classic style 'Round the houses' races, the Monaco Grand Prix has often been the first of the season's *Grandes Épreuves* in Europe. Even today, when it is usually anticipated by the Spanish Grand Prix in April, as well as the Argentinian and Brazilian events in January and the South African race in March, it has a special 'new season' atmosphere which attracts large numbers of visitors to Monte Carlo, especially British, who seem to be particularly appreciative of the carnival atmosphere.

The course winds through the streets, round the Casino square, along the promenade and harbour-side quays, and is a desperately tough event on cars and drivers alike, with well over a thousand gear changes and not a moment to relax in the concentrated two hours of racing. The Monaco Grand Prix has always been a race producing high drama and much heartbreak. Most people agree that, if a motor racing enthusiast could choose but a single race to attend in any one year, it should be the Monaco Grand Prix.

Monaco Grand Prix results

		Speed mph/kmh
1929	Williams (Bugatti)	49.83/80.19
1930	Dreyfus (Bugatti)	53.64/86.32
1931	Chiron (Bugatti)	54.10/87.06
1932	Nuvolari (Alfa Romeo)	55.91/89.82
1933	Varzi (Bugatti)	57.05/91.81
1934	Moll (Alfa Romeo)	56.05/90.20

		Speed mph/kmh
1935	Fagioli (Mercedes-Benz)	58.16/93.61
1936	Caracciola (Mercedes-Benz)	51.69/83.20
1937	Von Brauchitsch (Mercedes-Benz)	63.26/101.82
1948	Farina (Maserati)	59.74/96.15
1950	Fangio (Alfa Romeo)	61.33/98.70
1952	Marzotto (Ferrari)	58.20/93.66
1955	Trintignant (Ferrari)	65.81/105.91
1956	Moss (Maserati)	64.94/104.51
1957	Fangio (Maserati)	64.72/104.16
1958	Trintignant (Cooper)	67.99/109.41
1959	Brabham (Cooper)	66.71/107.36
1960	Moss (Lotus)	67.46/108.60
1961	Moss (Lotus)	70.70/113.79
1962	McLaren (Cooper)	70.46/113.40
1963	G. Hill (BRM)	72.43/116.56
1964	G. Hill (BRM)	72.64/116.91
1965	G. Hill (BRM)	74.34/119.64
1966	Stewart (BRM)	76.52/123.14
1967	Hulme (Brabham)	75.90/122.14
1968	G. Hill (Lotus)	77.82/125.24
1969	G. Hill (Lotus)	80.18/129.04
1970	Rindt (Lotus)	81.85/131.72
1971	Stewart (Tyrrell)	83.49/134.36
1972	Beltoise (BRM)	63.85/102.75
1973	Stewart (Tyrrell)	80.96/130.29
1974	Peterson (John Player Special)	80.75/129.94
1975	Lauda (Ferrari)	75.53/121.55

German Grand Prix

The German Grand Prix has been held at the Nür-burgring on all but three occasions and is notable for being a race where driver skill counts far more than in most other major events. Drivers are able to compensate for lack of power from their cars to a greater extent than in the majority of other top class races by getting round the proliferation of bends fractionally quicker than their opponents.

The Nürburgring is the longest circuit currently used in the world championship series. It is over 14 miles (22 km) long, with a great variety of bends and not many straights, yet it is quite a fast course which can be lapped at close to 120 mph (193 kmh).

Because of its character, it has produced many an heroic drive of which some of the best remembered are Nuvolari's incredible achievement in beating the might of the Mercedes-Benz and Auto-Union teams with a patently outpaced Alfa Romeo in 1935; Fangio's tremendous drive with a Maserati in 1957 when he broke the lap record repeatedly while chasing and passing the Ferraris of Hawthorn and Collins, following a pit stop; and Moss's great performance in beating the much more powerful Ferraris with a four-cylinder Lotus in 1961.

German Grand Prix results (at the Nürburgring, unless indicated otherwise):

		Speed mph/kmh
1926 (Avus)	Caracciola (Mercedes-Benz)	83.89/135.00
1927	Merz (Mercedes-Benz)	63.39/101.91
1928	Caracciola/Werner (Mercedes-Benz)	64.51/103.82
1929	Chiron (Bugatti)	66.38/106.86
1931	Caracciola (Mercedes-Benz)	67.26/108.24
1932	Caracciola (Alfa Romeo)	73.98/119.06
1934	Stück (Auto-Union)	76.39/122.93
1935	Nuvolari (Alfa Romeo)	75.25/121.10
1936	Rosemeyer (Auto-Union)	81.82/131.67
1937	Caracciola (Mercedes-Benz)	82.78/133.22
1938	Seaman (Mercedes-Benz)	80.72/129.90
1939	Caracciola (Mercedes-Benz)	75.25/121.10
1950	Ascari (Ferrari)	77.67/124.99
1951	Ascari (Ferrari)	83.76/134.79
1952	Ascari (Ferrari)	82.20/132.28
1953	Farina (Ferrari)	83.91/135.04
1954	Fangio (Mercedes-Benz)	82.77/133.20
1956	Fangio (Ferrari)	85.62/137.79
1957	Fangio (Maserati)	88.82/142.94
1958	Brooks (Vanwall)	90.31/145.34
1959 (Avus)	Brooks (Ferrari)	143.35/230.69
1960	Bonnier (Porsche)	80.28/129.19
1961	Moss (Lotus)	92.34/148.60
1962	G. Hill (BRM)	80.28/129.19
1963	Surtees (Ferrari)	95.83/154.22
1964	Surtees (Ferrari)	96.57/155.41
1965	Clark (Lotus)	99.79/160.59
1966	Brabham (Brabham)	86.74/139.59
1967	Hulme (Brabham)	101.47/163.30
1968	Stewart (Matra)	86.87/139.80
1969	Ickx (Brabham)	108.43/174.49
1970 (Hockenheim)	Rindt (Lotus)	123.90/199.39

		Speed mph/kmh
1971	Stewart (Tyrrell)	114.46/184.20
1972	Ickx (Ferrari)	116.63/187.69
1973	Stewart (Tyrrell)	116.82/188.00
1974	Regazzoni (Ferrari)	117.34/188.84
1975	Reutemann (Martini Brabham)	117.73/189.47

Spanish Grand Prix

The story of the Spanish Grand Prix is somewhat complicated as, until 1935, there were really two Spanish races of Grand Prix status, the Penya Rhin event at various circuits near Barcelona being of as much importance as a contemporary series of races at San Sebastian.

Although one of the most venerable races in the calendar, the Spanish Grand Prix has been held rather less consistently than most of the classics, due to the intervention of the Spanish Civil War and then, when local conditions might have made an international race in Spain feasible once more, World War II kept everybody else occupied.

Racing resumed in 1946 and continued rather irregularly until 1954 after which there was another lengthy gap, this time largely for financial reasons until, following an interval of fourteen years, the Spanish motor sport authorities produced two worthy circuits, at Madrid (Jarama) and Barcelona (Montjuich), between which the race has alternated since 1968.

Spanish Grand Prix results

		Speed mph/kmh
1921 (Villafranca)	Vizcaya (Bugatti)	53.02/85.33
1922 (Villafranca)	K. L. Guinness (Talbot-Darracq)	65.31/105.09
1923 (Sitges)	Divo (Sunbeam)	96.91/155.96
1923 (Villafranca)	Divo (Talbot-Darracq)	67.54/108.69

		Speed mph/kmh
1924 (San Sebastian)	Segrave (Sunbeam)	64.09/103.14
1925 (San Sebastian)	Divo (Delage)	76.40/122.95
1926 (San Sebastian)	Goux (Bugatti)	76.40/122.95
1927 (San Sebastian)	Benoist (Delage)	80.52/129.58
1928 (San Sebastian)	Chiron (Bugatti)	80.58/129.68
1929 (San Sebastian)	Varzi/Zehender (Alfa Romeo)	71.52/114.10
1930 (San Sebastian)	Varzi (Maserati)	86.82/139.72
1933 (San Sebastian)	Chiron (Alfa Romeo)	83.82/134.89
1933 (Montjuich)	Zanelli (Alfa Romeo)	59.10/95.11
1934 (San Sebastian)	Fagioli (Mercedes-Benz)	97.13/156.31
1934 (Montjuich)	Varzi (Alfa Romeo)	64.64/104.13
1935 (San Sebastian)	Caracciola (Mercedes-Benz)	102.40/164.79
1935 (Montjuich)	Fagioli (Mercedes-Benz)	66.99/107.81
1936 (Montjuich)	Nuvolari (Alfa Romeo)	69.20/111.36
1946 (Pedralbes)	Pelassa (Maserati)	80.25/129.15
1948 (Pedralbes)	Villoresi (Maserati)	89.44/143.94
1950 (Pedralbes)	Ascari (Ferrari)	94.10/151.44
1951 (Pedralbes)	Fangio (Alfa Romeo)	98.76/158.93
1954 (Pedralbes)	Hawthorn (Ferrari)	97.99/157.70
1968 (Jarama)	Hill (Lotus)	84.40/135.84
1969 (Montjuich)	Stewart (Matra)	92.91/149.52
1970 (Jarama)	Stewart (March)	87.21/140.36
1971 (Montjuich)	Stewart (Tyrrell)	97.19/156.41
1972 (Jarama)	Fittipaldi (John Player Special)	92.35/148.63
1973 (Montjuich)	Fittipaldi (John Player Special)	97.86/157.49
1974 (Jarama)	Lauda (Ferrari)	88.47/142.40
1975 (Montjuich)	Mass (Texaco-Marlboro)	95.56/153.76

British Grand Prix

Coming, as it does these days, about two-thirds of the way through the world championship, the British Grand Prix often plays a vital part in the series and there is a three to one chance that the driver who comes first or second will be that year's World Champion.

Ignoring the two relatively unimportant Brooklands races in the twenties and the two Donington Grand Prix events of the thirties, the British Grand Prix has been held at three venues: Silverstone, Aintree and Brands Hatch.

There have been many memorable races, but three deserving special mention are the Ferrari win by Gonzales at Silverstone in 1951, the first time that Ferrari beat the Alfa Romeo team in a straight fight; Stirling Moss's Mercedes-Benz victory at Aintree in 1955 (the first success by a British driver in the world championship series); and the Moss/Brooks win for Vanwall, again at Aintree, two years later, which was the first modern GP victory for a British car and heralded the near-domination of Formula 1 racing by British-built cars and engines which has lasted to the present time.

British Grand Prix results

		Speed mph/kmh
1948 (Silverstone)	Villoresi (Maserati)	72.28/116.32
1949 (Silverstone)	de Graffenried (Maserati)	77.31/124.41
1950 (Silverstone)	Farina (Alfa Romeo)	90.95/145.37
1951 (Silverstone)	Gonzales (Ferrari)	96.11/154.67
1952 (Silverstone)	Ascari (Ferrari)	90.92/146.32
1953 (Silverstone)	Ascari (Ferrari)	92.97/149.62
1954 (Silverstone)	Gonzales (Ferrari)	89.69/144.34

		Speed mph/kmh
1955 (Aintree)	Moss (Mercedes-Benz)	86.47/139.16
1956 (Silverstone)	Fangio (Ferrari)	98.65/158.76
1957 (Aintree)	Moss/Brooks (Vanwall)	86.80/139.69
1958 (Silverstone)	Collins (Ferrari)	102.05/164.23
1959 (Aintree)	Brabham (Cooper)	89.88/134.64
1960 (Silverstone)	Brabham (Cooper)	108.69/174.91
1961 (Aintree)	von Trips (Ferrari)	83.91/135.04
1962 (Aintree)	Clark (Lotus)	92.25/148.56
1963 (Silverstone)	Clark (Lotus)	107.75/173.40
1964 (Brands Hatch)	Clark (Lotus)	94.14/151.50
1965 (Silverstone)	Clark (Lotus)	112.02/180.27
1966 (Brands Hatch)	Brabham (Brabham)	95.48/153.66
1967 (Silverstone)	Clark (Lotus)	117.64/189.32
1968 (Brands Hatch)	Siffert (Lotus)	104.83/168.70
1969 (Silverstone)	Stewart (Matra)	127.25/204.78
1970 (Brands Hatch)	Rindt (Lotus)	108.69/174.91
1971 (Silverstone)	Stewart (Tyrrell)	130.48/209.98
1972 (Brands Hatch)	Fittipaldi (John Player Special)	112.06/180.34
1973 (Silverstone)	Revson (McLaren)	131.75/212.03
1974 (Brands Hatch)	Scheckter (Tyrrell)	115.73/186.24
1975 (Silverstone)	Fittipaldi (Texaco-Marlboro)	120.01/193.15

Dutch Grand Prix

Unique among the classic races in having always been held on precisely the same circuit – at the North Sea resort of Zandvoort – the Dutch Grand Prix therefore has greater continuity than all the rest.

The circuit is built among the sand dunes and

the race is usually held before the start of the holiday summer season so that local hotels can provide ample accommodation for the racegoers.

The Dutch Grand Prix has specially happy memories for British racing enthusiasts. The very first race, in 1948, was an invitation event to the British Racing Drivers Club, signifying the esteem in which the Dutch people held the British after World War II and it was won by the Siamese Prince 'Bira', who based his motor racing activities in the UK. The Dutch race gave BRM their very first Grand Prix win (in 1959) and the same team the first GP success of their world championship year (1962). It was also the scene of the very first appearance (and victory) of the Ford Cosworth DFV engine, in Clark's Lotus, in 1967.

Dutch Grand Prix results

		Speed mph/kmh
1948	'Bira' (Maserati)	73.25/117.88
1949	Villoresi (Ferrari)	77.10/124.06
1950	Rosier (Talbot)	76.45/123.32
1951	Rosier (Talbot)	78.40/126.26
1952	Ascari (Ferrari)	81.05/130.42
1953	Ascari (Ferrari)	80.99/130.35
1955	Fangio (Mercedes-Benz)	89.65/144.27
1958	Moss (Vanwall)	93.65/151.16
1959	Bonnier (BRM)	93.46/150.41
1960	Brabham (Cooper)	96.27/154.93
1961	von Trips (Ferrari)	96.21/154.83
1962	G. Hill (BRM)	95.44 153.53
1963	Clark (Lotus)	97.53/156.96
1964	Clark (Lotus)	98.02/157.75
1965	Clark (Lotus)	100.86/162.33
1966	Brabham (Brabham)	100.09/161.09
1967	Clark (Lotus)	104.38/168.09
1968	Stewart (Matra)	84.66/136.25
1969	Stewart (Matra)	111.04/178.71
1970	Rindt (Lotus)	112.96/181.78
1971	Ickx (Ferrari)	94.06/151.37
1973	Stewart (Tyrrell)	114.35/184.03
1974	Lauda (Ferrari)	114.72/184.64
1975	Hunt (Hesketh)	110.48/177.77

The Tourist Trophy

Initiated as a test for standard cars, the Tourist Trophy race has now gone the full circle and is once again for standard production saloons. It is the oldest motor race in the calendar, starting in 1905.

However, there have been numerous and lengthy intervals in the race's continuity, particularly in the Isle of Man series (where it started) before and after World War I.

Then came the first of the races on open road circuits in Northern Ireland (on the Ards circuit) where the TT stayed and created its great reputation, prior to two years on the English mainland, at Donington Park (1937-8). It resumed in Ulster (on the Dundrod circuit) in 1950, in a period when sports cars became two-seater racing cars. A serious accident in 1955 (the same year as the Le Mans tragedy) cast doubts on Dundrod's suitability and it was three years before the TT was held again, from then on using closed tracks in England.

The Goodwood races (1958-64) were mostly sports car or Grand Touring championship events. Oulton Park was used for more sports car races (1965-9) and, since 1970, the TT has been for saloons at Silverstone.

Tourist Trophy Race results

			Speed mph/kmh
1905	(Isle of Man)	Napier (Arrol-Johnston)	33.90/54.55
1906	(Isle of Man)	Rolls (Rolls-Royce)	39.60/63.73
1907	(Isle of Man)	Courtis (Rover)	28.80/46.35
1908	(Isle of Man)	Watson (Hutton)	50.25/80.87
1914	(Isle of Man)	K. Lee Guinness (Sunbeam)	56.44/90.83
1922	(Isle of Man)	Chassagne (Sunbeam)	55.70/89.64
1928	(Ards)	Don (Lea-Francis)	64.06/103.09
1929	(Ards)	Caracciola (Mercedes-Benz)	72.82/117.19
1930	(Ards)	Nuvolari (Alfa Romeo)	70.88/114.07
1931	(Ards)	Black (MG)	67.90/109.27
1932	(Ards)	Whitcroft (Riley)	74.23/119.46
1933	(Ards)	Nuvolari (MG)	78.65/126.57
1934	(Ards)	Dodson (MG)	74.65/120.13

			Speed mph/kmh
1935	(Ards)	Dixon (Riley)	76.90/123.76
1936	(Ards)	Dixon/Dodson (Riley)	78.01/125.54
1937	(Donington)	Comotti (Talbot Darracq)	68.70/110.56
1938	(Donington)	Gerard (Delage)	67.61/108.80
1950	(Dundrod)	Moss (Jaguar)	75.15/120.94
1951	(Dundrod)	Moss (Jaguar)	83.55/134.46
1953	(Dundrod)	Collins/Griffith (Aston Martin)	81.71/131.50
1954	(Dundrod)	Laureau/Armagnac (Panhard)	68.75/110.64
1955	(Dundrod)	Moss/Fitch (Mercedes-Benz)	88.32/142.13
1958	(Goodwood)	Moss/Brooks (Aston Martin)	88.33/142.15
1959	(Goodwood)	Moss/Shelby/Fairman (Aston Martin)	89.41/143.89
1960	(Goodwood)	Moss (Ferrari)	85.58/137.72
1961	(Goodwood)	Moss (Ferrari)	86.62/139.40
1962	(Goodwood)	Ireland (Ferrari)	94.05/151.35
1963	(Goodwood)	G. Hill (Ferrari)	95.14/153.11
1964	(Goodwood)	G. Hill (Ferrari)	97.13/156.31
1965	(Oulton Park)	Hulme (Brabham)	94.07/151.42
1966	(Oulton Park)	Hulme (Lola)	94.21/151.61
1967	(Oulton Park)	de Adamich (Alfa Romeo)	84.66/136.24
1968	(Oulton Park)	Hulme (Lola)	99.06/159.42
1969	(Oulton Park)	T. Taylor (Lola)	96.86/155.88
1970	(Silverstone)	Muir (Chevrolet)	99.94/160.83
1972	(Silverstone)	Mass/Glemser (Ford)	106.53/171.44
1973	(Silverstone)	Ertl/Bell (BMW)	108.78/175.06
1974	(Silverstone)	Graham (Chevrolet)	96.87/155.89

The Targa Florio

Founded in 1906, the Targa Florio in Sicily has been both one of the greatest and certainly the longest-surviving of open road events but now this aspect has been extinguished. Some of the races have been round the entire coastline of Sicily – some 670 miles (1,078 km) – while what has been known as the 'Short' Madonie circuit was used after 1931 and was a mere 45 miles (72 km)!

The roads have been closed to other traffic but otherwise completely natural with villages, kerbs, stone walls, precipices, trees, etc., to mark the edge of the track. Equally, animals and pedestrians have strayed onto the course with little hindrance and it has been left to the island's population to use their own sense of self-preservation to decide how close to the edge to stand and in what position.

Innumerable bends and hardly any significant straights have made this an immensely tough contest for both cars and drivers, and (apart from a short period when the race was held on a closed circuit in a park) it was not until after World War II that race average speeds first exceeded 50 mph (80 kmh). The last race was in 1973.

Targa Florio results

		Speed mph/kmh
1906 (Long Madonie)	Cagno (Itala)	29.07/46.78
1907 (Long Madonie)	Nazzaro (Fiat)	33.40/53.75
1908 (Long Madonie)	Trucco (Isotta Fraschini)	37.20/59.87
1909 (Long Madonie)	Ciuppa (Spa)	34.00/54.72
1910 (Long Madonie)	Cariolato (Franco)	29.19/46.98
1911 (Long Madonie)	Ceirano (SCAT)	29.10/46.83
1912 (Circuit of Sicily)	Snipe/Pardini (SCAT)	24.30/39.11
1913 (Circuit of Sicily)	Nazzaro (Nazzaro)	31.04/49.95
1914 (Circuit of Sicily)	Ceirano (SCAT)	38.94/62.67
1919 (Medium Madonie)	Boillot (Peugeot)	34.19/55.02
1920 (Medium Madonie)	Meregalli (Nazzaro)	31.70/51.01
1921 (Medium Madonie)	Masetti (Fiat)	36.20/58.26
1922 (Medium Madonie)	Masetti (Mercedes-Benz)	39.20/63.08
1923 (Medium Madonie)	Sivocci (Alfa Romeo)	36.70/59.06
1924 (Medium Madonie)	Werner (Mercedes-Benz)	41.02/66.01
1925 (Medium Madonie)	Constantini (Bugatti)	44.48/71.58
1926 (Medium Madonie)	Constantini (Bugatti)	45.77/73.66

		Speed mph/kmh
1927 (Medium Madonie)	Materassi (Bugatti)	44.15/71.05
1928 (Medium Madonie)	Divo (Bugatti)	45.65/73.46
1929 (Medium Madonie)	Divo (Bugatti)	46.20/74.35
1930 (Medium Madonie)	Varzi (Alfa Romeo)	48.50/78.05
1931 (Big Madonie)	Nuvolari (Alfa Romeo)	40.28/64.82
1932 (Short Madonie)	Nuvolari (Alfa Romeo)	49.30/79.34
1933 (Short Madonie)	Brivio (Alfa Romeo)	47.50/76.44
1934 (Short Madonie)	Varzi (Alfa Romeo)	43.01/69.22
1935 (Short Madonie)	Brivio (Alfa Romeo)	49.18/79.15
1936 (Short Madonie)	Magistri (Lancia)	41.69/67.09
1937 (Favorita Park)	Severi (Maserati)	66.90/107.66
1938 (Favorita Park)	Rocco (Maserati)	71.00/114.26
1939 (Favorita Park)	Villoresi (Maserati)	84.70/136.31
1940 (Favorita Park)	Villoresi (Maserati)	88.40/142.26
1948 (Circuit of Sicily)	Biondetti/Igor (Ferrari)	55.20/88.83
1949 (Circuit of Sicily)	Biondetti/Benedetti (Ferrari)	51.35/82.64
1950 (Circuit of Sicily)	Bornigia/Bornigia (Alfa Romeo)	54.00/86.90
1951 (Short Madonie)	Cortese (Frazer-Nash)	47.50/76.44
1952 (Short Madonie)	Bonetto (Lancia)	49.70/79.98
1953 (Short Madonie)	Maglioli (Lancia)	50.09/80.61
1954 (Short Madonie)	Taruffi (Lancia)	55.80/89.80
1955 (Short Madonie)	Moss/Collins (Mercedes-Benz)	59.80/96.24
1956 (Short Madonie)	Maglioli/Von Hanstein (Porsche)	56.50/90.93
1958 (Short Madonie)	Musso/Gendebien (Ferrari)	58.91/94.80
1959 (Short Madonie)	Barth/Seidel (Porsche)	56.74/91.31
1960 (Short Madonie)	Bonnier/Herrmann (Porsche)	59.00/94.95
1961 (Short Madonie)	von Trips/Gendebien (Ferrari)	64.10/103.16

		Speed mph/kmh
1962 (Short Madonie)	Mairesse/Rodriguez/Gendebien (Ferrari)	63.30/101.87
1963 (Short Madonie)	Bonnier/Abate (Porsche)	64.41/103.66
1964 (Short Madonie)	Pucci/Davis (Porsche)	61.48/98.94
1965 (Short Madonie)	Vaccarella/Bandini (Ferrari)	62.28/100.23
1966 (Short Madonie)	Mairesse/Muller (Porsche)	63.73/102.56
1967 (Short Madonie)	Hawkins/Stommelen (Porsche)	67.61/108.80
1968 (Short Madonie)	Elford/Maglioli (Porsche)	75.25/121.10
1969 (Short Madonie)	Mitter/Schütze (Porsche)	72.99/117.46
1970 (Short Madonie)	Siffert/Redman (Porsche)	75.50/121.50
1971 (Short Madonie)	Vaccarella/Hezemans (Alfa Romeo)	74.63/120.10
1972 (Short Madonie)	Merzario/Munari (Ferrari)	76.14/122.53
1973 (Short Madonie)	Van Lennep/Muller (Porsche)	71.27/114.59

Mille Miglia

A 1,000-mile (1,609-km) sports car race on public roads, from Brescia, down the Adriatic coast, across to Rome and then back up to Brescia, the Mille Miglia was a race of great tradition, nearly always run in the same manner. Cars were started at one-minute intervals, their numbers corresponding to their starting-time (e.g., No. 555 set off at 5.55 a.m.).

Another tradition, that 'He who leads at Rome, never wins the Mille Miglia' was proved a myth only in 1955, when Stirling Moss won the fastest-ever race.

The Mille Miglia was an immense challenge to man and machine, and most cars were driven by two men, taking turns at the wheel. The first winner to do it single-handed was the great Nuvolari; most later victors did not share the driving, although few went without a passenger.

Crowd control was always difficult and, inevitably, there was a terrible slaughter when, in 1957, the Spaniard, the Marquis de Portago, ploughed into the spectators, dying among them, which caused the race to be abandoned.

Mille Miglia results (Brescia–Rome–Brescia, except 1940, which was nine laps of Brescia–Cremona–Brescia)

		Speed mph/kmh
1927	Minoia/Morandi (O.M.)	47.80/76.92
1928	Campari Ramponi (Alfa Romeo)	52.14/83.91
1929	Campari/Ramponi (Alfa Romeo)	54.99/88.49
1930	Nuvolari/Guidotti (Alfa Romeo)	62.41/100.44
1931	Caracciola/Sebastian (Mercedes-Benz)	62.85/101.14
1932	Borzacchini/Bignami (Alfa Romeo)	67.72/108.98
1933	Nuvolari (Alfa Romeo)	67.50/108.63
1934	Varzi/Bignami (Alfa Romeo)	71.21/114.60
1935	Pintacuda/della Stuffa (Alfa Romeo)	71.72/115.42
1936	Brivio/Ongaro (Alfa Romeo)	75.57/121.61
1937	Pintacuda/Mambelli (Alfa Romeo)	71.31/114.76
1938	Biondetti/Stefani (Alfa Romeo)	84.13/135.39
1940	Baümer/Von Hanstein (BMW)	103.59/166.71
1947	Biondetti (Alfa Romeo)	69.58/111.98
1948	Biondetti/Igor (Ferrari)	75.14/120.92
1949	Biondetti/Salami (Ferrari)	81.53/131.21
1950	Marzotto (Ferrari)	76.79/123.58
1951	Villoresi (Ferrari)	75.52/121.53
1952	Bracco (Ferrari)	79.74/128.33
1953	Marzotto (Ferrari)	88.28/142.07
1954	Ascari (Lancia)	86.69/139.51
1955	Moss (Mercedes-Benz)	97.93/157.60
1956	Castellotti (Ferrari)	85.38/137.40
1957	Taruffi (Ferrari)	94.83/152.61

No longer practised, the Le Mans start (seen here at Le Mans itself) tested both cockpit access and driver agility

Le Mans 24-hour Race

Arguably the world's most famous and prestigious motor race, the Le Mans 24-hours is rightly called 'Le Grand Prix d'Endurance'. It began in 1923 as a proving event for production-type sports cars but, as with so many other attempts to maintain a resemblance to everyday motoring, the race eventually reverted to cars built specially for the purpose.

After World War II, the event reached new heights of popularity, although the essential character changed little. The organizers also used an Index of Performance award relating distance to engine size) and sometimes an Index of Thermal Efficiency (relating fuel consumption to performance).

The series was jeopardized by the world's worst motor racing disaster when, in 1955, the Mercedes-Benz of 'Levegh' plunged into the crowd and over 80 died. Many races throughout the world were cancelled as a consequence but, next year, the '24-hours' went on again, with a revised pit area.

Crowds of around a quarter-million attend, with a full-sized fairground and other side-attractions to provide a remarkable atmosphere.

108

Le Mans 24-hour Race results

		Speed mph/kmh
1923	Lagache/Leonard (Chenard-Walcker)	57.21/92.07
1924	Duff/Clement (Bentley)	53.78/86.55
1925	de Courcelles/Rossignol (Lorraine)	57.85/93.10
1926	Bloch/Rossignol (Lorraine)	66.08/106.34
1927	Benjafield/Davis (Bentley)	61.35/98.73
1928	Barnato/Rubin (Bentley)	69.11/111.22
1929	Barnato/Birkin (Bentley)	73.63/118.49
1930	Barnato/Kidston (Bentley)	75.88/121.11
1931	Howe/Birkin (Alfa Romeo)	78.13/125.73
1932	Sommer/Chinetti (Alfa Romeo)	76.49/123.10
1933	Sommer/Nuvolari (Alfa Romeo)	81.40/131.00
1934	Chinetti/Etancelin (Alfa Romeo)	74.75/120.30
1935	Hindmarsh/Fontes (Lagonda)	77.85/125.28
1937	Wimille/Benoist (Bugatti)	85.13/137.00
1938	Chaboud/Tremoulet (Delahaye)	82.36/132.54
1939	Wimille/Veyron (Bugatti)	86.60/139.37
1949	Chinetti/Selsdon (Ferrari)	82.27/132.40
1950	Rosier/Rosier (Talbot-Darracq)	89.73/144.40
1951	Walker/Whitehead (Jaguar)	93.49/150.45
1952	Lang/Reiss (Mercedes-Benz)	96.67/155.57
1953	Rolt/Hamilton (Jaguar)	105.85/170.34
1954	Gonzales/Trinignant (Ferrari)	105.15/169.22
1955	Hawthorn/Bueb (Jaguar)	107.07/172.31
1956	Flockhart/Sanderson (Jaguar)	104.46/168.11
1957	Flockhart/Bueb (Jaguar)	113.85/183.22
1958	Gendebien/P. Hill (Ferrari)	106.12/170.78
1959	Salvadori/Shelby (Aston Martin)	112.57/181.16
1960	Frere/Gendebien (Ferrari)	109.19/175.72
1961	P. Hill/Gendebien (Ferrari)	115.60/186.04
1962	P. Hill/Gendebien (Ferrari)	114.90/184.91
1963	Scarfiotti/Bandini (Ferrari)	118.11/189.82
1964	Guichet/Vaccarella (Ferrari)	121.55/196.61
1965	Gregory/Rindt (Ferrari)	121.09/194.87
1966	McLaren/Amon (Ford)	125.49/201.95
1967	Foyt/Gurney (Ford)	135.48/218.03
1968	Rodriguez/Bianchi (Ford)	114.93/184.96
1969	Ickx/Oliver (Ford)	129.40/208.24
1970	Attwood/Herrmann (Porsche)	119.30/191.99
1971	Marko/Van Lennep (Porsche)	138.13/222.29
1972	G. Hill/Pescarolo (Matra-Simca)	121.39/195.35
1973	Pescarolo/Larrousse (Matra-Simca)	125.60/202.12
1974	Pescarolo/Larrousse (Matra-Simca)	119.00/191.51
1975	Bell/Ickx (Gulf)	119.01/191.48

Indianapolis 500

Nowadays the richest race in the world, worth more to the winner than an entire season of Grand Prix racing, the Indianapolis 500-mile (804-km) race has more tradition than possibly any other. Most of the time it has been almost purely an American event but, in its early days, again in the 1940s and finally in the sixties, European cars 'invaded' Indianapolis with great success.

In the fifties, the regular contestants had brought to a relatively high degree of efficiency the front-engined, Offenhauser-powered 'roadster' type car with off-set suspension thought to be essential to negotiate at the required speed the four 90 degree turns of the rectangular 2½-mile (4-km) track (originally paved with over three million bricks, hence the nickname 'Brickyard'). Following Jim Clark's win in a rear-engined Lotus in 1965, which should have been predictable after Jack Brabham's attempt in 1961 with a Cooper, every subsequent 'Indy' winner has conformed to the basic layout of the modern European-type Grand Prix car.

Renowned for its immense speed and its spectacular crashes, Indianapolis also has its own unique system of qualification, requiring weeks of intensive practice and time trials.

Indianapolis '500' results

		Speed mph/kmh
1911	Harroun (Marmon Wasp)	74.59/120.04
1912	Dawson (National)	78.72/126.68
1913	Goux (Peugeot)	75.93/122.19
1914	Thomas (Delage)	82.47/132.72
1915	de Palma (Mercedes)	89.84/144.58
1916	Resta (Peugeot)	84.00/135.18
1919	Wilcox (Peugeot)	88.05/141.70
1920	Chevrolet (Monroe)	88.62/142.62
1921	Milton (Frontenac)	89.62/144.23
1922	Murphy (Murphy Special)	94.48/152.05

		Speed mph/kmh
1923	Milton (HCS Spl.)	90.95/146.37
1924	Corum/Boyer (Duesenberg Spl.)	98.23/158.08
1925	de Paolo (Duesenberg Spl.)	101.13/162.75
1926	Lockhart (Miller Spl.)	95.90/154.33
1927	Souders (Duesenberg)	97.55/156.99
1928	Meyer (Miller Spl.)	99.48/160.09
1929	Keech (Simplex Piston Ring Spl.)	97.59/157.05
1930	Arnold (Miller Hartz Spl.)	100.45/161.65
1931	Schneider (Bowes Seal Fast Spl.)	96.63/155.51
1932	Frame (Miller Hartz Spl.)	104.14/167.59
1933	Meyer (Tydol Spl.)	104.16/167.62
1934	Cummings (Boyle Spl.)	104.86/168.75
1935	Petillo (Gilmore Spl.)	106.20/170.91
1936	Meyer (Ring Free Spl.)	109.06/175.51
1937	Shaw (Gilmore Spl.)	113.58/182.78
1938	Roberts (Burd Piston Ring Spl.)	117.20/188.61
1939	Shaw (Boyle Spl.)	115.04/185.13
1940	Shaw (Boyle Spl.)	114.28/183.91
1941	Rose/Davis (Hose Clamp Spl.)	115.12/185.26
1946	Robson (Thorne Spl.)	114.82/184.78
1947	Rose (Blue Crown Spark Plug Spl.)	116.34/187.23
1948	Rose (Blue Crown Spark Plug Spl.)	119.81/192.81
1949	Holland (Blue Crown Spark Plug Spl.)	121.33/195.26
1950	Parsons (Kurtis-Kraft)	124.00/199.55
1951	Wallard (Belanger Spl.)	126.24/203.16
1952	Ruttman (Agajanian Spl.)	128.92/207.47
1953	Vukovich (Fuel Injection Spl.)	128.74/207.18
1954	Vukovich (Fuel Injection Spl.)	130.84/210.56
1955	Sweikert (John Zink Spl.)	128.21/206.33
1956	Flaherty (John Zink Spl.)	128.49/206.78
1957	Hanks (Belond Exhaust Spl.)	135.60/218.22
1958	Bryan (Belond AP)	133.79/215.31
1959	Ward (Leader Card Spl.)	135.86/218.64
1960	Rathmann (Ken Paul Spl.)	138.77/223.32
1961	Foyt (Bowes Seal Fast Spl.)	139.13/223.90
1962	Ward (Leader Card 500 Roadster Spl.)	140/29/225.77
1963	Jones (Agajanian Willard Battery Spl.)	143.13/233.56
1964	Foyt (Sheraton Thompson Spl.)	147.35/237.13
1965	Clark (Lotus Ford)	150.68/242.49
1966	Hill (American Red Ball Spl.)	144.31/232.24
1967	Foyt (Coyote Ford)	151.21/243.34
1968	R. Unser (Eagle Offenhauser)	152.88/246.03
1969	Andretti (Hawk Ford)	156.87/252.45
1970	A. Unser (Colt Ford)	156.75/252.26
1971	A. Unser (Colt Ford)	157.73/253.83
1972	Donohue (McLaren Offenhauser)	163.46/263.06
1973	Johncock (Eagle Offenhauser)	159.02/255.81
1974	Rutherford (McLaren Offenhauser)	158.59/255.22
1975	R. Unser (Eagle Offenhauser)	149.21/239.08

7: GREAT RACING DRIVERS

Camille Jenatzy (Belgium), 1868–1913 The 'Red Devil' was a former cycle racer and a civil engineer. A regular and highly successful driver in the long-distance races of the turn of the century, he won the 1903 Gordon-Bennett Cup in Ireland and was second in 1904 in Germany (both for Mercedes). He died in a hunting accident.

He was also one of the earliest record-breakers for the world's fastest speed in a car, conducting a great duel with the Comte de Chasseloup-Laubat. He used electric cars and set a long-standing 65.79 mph (105.86 kmh) record in 1899 with the cigar-shaped 'Le Jamais Content'.

Felice Nazzaro (Italy), 1881–1940 A FIAT apprentice who became their greatest racing driver. He was also at one time chauffeur to Vincenzo Florio, the sportsman who sponsored him in many races as well as founding the Coppa Florio and Targa Florio races, both of which Nazzaro was to win. During 1907 he won the Targa, the French Grand Prix and the Kaiserpreis, all for FIAT.

When they withdrew from racing, he built and raced his own cars successfully. FIAT's return in 1922 brought him back to the fold and he won the French Grand Prix at the age of 41. He became their competition manager and continued until the time of his death.

Georges Boillot (France), 1885–1916 The hero of France before, and during, World War I, he began racing in 1908 with a Lion-Peugeot. In 1909 he won the Normandie Cup and in 1910 the voi-

Camille Jenatzy

Georges Boillot

turette class of the Targa Florio. After numerous high placings he won the 1912 French Grand Prix with the new Ernest Henry Peugeot, and repeated this win and took the Coupe de l'Auto in 1913.

Boillot is best remembered for his titanic struggle with the Mercedes team in the 1914 French Grand Prix, finally succumbing with mechanical trouble. In the war, he became a pilot and was shot down over the Western Front.

Achille Varzi (Italy), 1904–1948 Nuvolari's great rival, Varzi, came from a wealthy family and was noted for his cool, calculated driving and grim expression. He began with motorcycles and raced against Nuvolari, but teamed up with him in Bugatti cars in 1928. Nuvolari kept winning so Varzi went. This happened in several subsequent teams.

He won many races in the 1930s (seven major events in 1934) and was very successful with Auto-Union in 1936 but, in 1937, he began taking drugs and did little racing until 1946, when he joined Alfa Romeo and had several wins. He died in an accident while practising for the Swiss Grand Prix.

Tazio Nuvolari

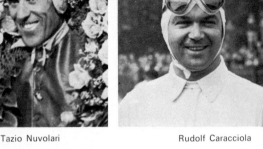

Rudolf Caracciola

Tazio Nuvolari (Italy), 1892–1953 Known as the 'Flying Mantuan', he was possibly the greatest driver of all. He raced cycles, motorcycles and finally cars, from 1920. An indefatigable little man who, more than once, ignored recent serious injuries to race again, bandaged and splinted.

He scored innumerable wins in all the great races throughout the world, in the twenties and thirties, in all types of car. This included five Grands Prix, the Mille Miglia, Le Mans and the TT in one (1933) season, while his 1935 German Grand Prix win over Mercedes and Auto-Union with an out-dated Alfa Romeo is legendary. He continued to race after the war until ill-health forced retirement.

Rudolf Caracciola (Germany), 1901–1959 He began racing cars in 1922 and, apart from short periods when they withdrew, after 1923 raced only for Mercedes-Benz. He was known alternately as 'Bergmeister' and 'Regenmeister' for his domination respectively of hillclimbs and wet races. His first major track success was the 1926 German Grand Prix.

In 1932, with Alfa Romeo, he won four major races but broke his thigh badly in 1933 and suffered pain ever after. Caracciola enjoyed great success with Mercedes-Benz in 750 kilogram formula (including five GP wins in both 1935 and 1937). He raced again after the war but bad accidents stopped his career.

Hermann Lang (Germany), 1909– He began racing in 1935 for Mercedes-Benz, after being a mechanic for them, and started winning from 1937 (Avus Grand Prix at 162.61 mph (261.72 kmh) – the fastest GP until then). He had two more GP wins in 1938 before his greatest season with five GPs (Tripoli, Pau, Eifel, Belgium and Switzerland) to become European champion as well as German Hill climb Champion.

Lang resumed racing after the war, winning Le Mans 24-hour and Nürburgring 1,000 kilometres of 1952 and raced again with the Grand Prix Mercedes-Benz team in 1954.

Giuseppe Farina (Italy), 1909–1966 'Nino' Farina was the first world champion (1950) and a smooth, stylish but bad-tempered driver. One of the Farina coachbuilding family, he was also a Doctor of Law. Befriended and encouraged by Nuvolari, he joined Alfa Romeo in 1936 and was Italian champion in 1938 and 1939.

He resumed his connection with Alfa Romeo in 1946 and won the German Grand Prix. With Maserati in 1948, he won four major races. When Alfa Romeo came back in 1950, he won the British, Italian and Swiss rounds to take the world championship. He was killed in a road accident on his way to a motor race.

Juan Manuel Fangio (Argentina), 1911– Certainly the most successful Grand Prix driver of the post-war years and perhaps of all time. He began in the early town-to-town races in South America but went to Europe in 1949 and won numerous races with Maserati.

Next season, with Alfa Romeo, he was runner-up in the world championship and won the 1951 championship, also gaining the title in 1954, 1955, 1956 and 1957 for Maserati, Ferrari and Mercedes-Benz. It was almost impossible to beat him in a competitive car and it was said of him, 'The easiest way to win the world championship is to hire Fangio'. Now a Mercedes-Benz importer to Argentina.

Alberto Ascari (Italy), 1918–1955 Son of the famous driver Antonio Ascari (killed when Alberto was seven), he raced motorcycles before driving Ferrari's first car in 1940. After considerable success with Maseratis in 1947/48, he rejoined Ferrari in 1949, to gradually overcome the Alfa Romeo dominance.

He was almost unrivalled in 1952/53, winning the championship both years. In 1954 he won the Mille Miglia with a Lancia, and in 1955 he was leading the Monaco Grand Prix for them when he crashed into the harbour. Still unfit through minor injuries,

Giuseppe Farina   Alberto Ascari

Stirling Moss   Mike Hawthorn

he was killed four days later in an inexplicable practice crash with a Ferrari sports car.

Stirling Moss (Great Britain), 1929–   The best
post-war driver never to win the world championship. He started in 1948 in 500 cc cars, dominating
this class. He went on to Formula 2, the world
championship category of 1952/53.

In 1955 he joined Mercedes-Benz to win Mille
Miglia, Targa Florio and the British Grand Prix –
the first British driver to do so. With Brooks in Vanwall, he was the first to win the British Grand Prix
in a British car (1957). Many more GP wins in 1956
(Maserati), 1957/8 (Vanwall – with manufacturers'
championship), 1959 (Cooper) 1960/1 (Lotus).
Seven TT wins, etc., before a serious crash at
Goodwood (1962) caused his retirement.

**Mike Hawthorn (Great Britain), 1929–
1959**   Perhaps the most immediately successful
driver and the first British world champion. He
began racing in 1951 with Riley sports cars and in
the second season was given a chance in the new

Cooper Bristol Formula 2. Overcoming the car's inherent shortcomings with many fine drives, he was asked to join Ferrari for 1953, when he won a famous victory over Fangio in a side-by-side battle at the French Grand Prix.

He won at Le Mans in 1955 (Jaguar) but had poor Grand Prix years then and subsequently with Vanwall and BRM. He rejoined Ferrari in 1957 and won 1958 championship with the French Grand Prix win and numerous seconds. He retired at the end of the season, but was killed within months in a road accident.

C.A.S. (Tony) Brooks (Great Britain), 1932–
The first to take British Formula 1 car to an international Grand Prix win for over 30 years (Connaught at 1955 Syracuse Grand Prix). He began in British sports car club races. After the Syracuse win, he joined BRM for 1956 but, after a disappointing season went to Vanwall, sharing with Moss the 1957 British Grand Prix triumph at Aintree.

He had three GP wins in 1958, helping Vanwall to manufacturers' championship, and two more for Ferrari in 1959, when he was runner-up to Brabham in the drivers' championship. He retired in 1961 after two less successful seasons.

Jack Brabham (Australia), 1926–
The first man to win a Grand Prix (and the world championship) in a car of his own make. After midget dirt track racing in Australia, he came to England in 1955. He joined Cooper in 1957 and enjoyed Formula 2 successes. In 1959 and 1960 he won world championships for Cooper and then set up his own factory.

Although his cars were successful for others, he had to wait until 1966 for another win himself. With 3-litre Australian Repco engine for new formula, he

Tony Brooks

Jack Brabham

won the championship a third time. Two more GP wins in 1967 when his team-mate Hulme was champion. He retired in 1970 after further GP wins.

Jim Clark (Great Britain), 1936–1968 Up to the time of his death, the most successful Formula 1 driver with 25 Grand Prix wins and two world championships (1963 and 1965). Also the first Briton to win Indianapolis 500 (1965) and one of the most prolific race winners of all time, nearly always in Lotus cars.

A Scottish farmer who began racing in 1956, Clark was also one of the most modest and universally respected drivers. As well as two championships, he was runner-up in 1962 and 1964, losing in the final round both times. He died in a crash in a minor Formula 2 race.

Phil Hill (USA), 1927– To date, he is North America's only world champion driver, but more successful in sports car racing, winning the Le Mans 24-hour race three times, the Sebring 12-hour three times and the Nürburgring 1,000 kilometres twice.

Jim Clark

Phil Hill

After an early career in American sports car races, he joined Ferrari in 1956 and most successes were with them. His driver's championship was in 1961, a season of near-domination by Ferrari and was settled when his team-mate, the German Wolfgang von Trips, was killed in the Italian Grand Prix. Hill continued to win major sports car races up to 1967.

Graham Hill (Great Britain), 1929– The only driver ever to have won the world championship, Indianapolis 500 and Le Mans. He began five years with Lotus in 1956 without outstanding success. He went to BRM and took the world championship in 1962. He won two Grands Prix in each of the following three years and (in Lola) the 1966 Indianapolis 500. Back to Lotus in 1967 with Clark. In 1968, following Clark's death, he led Lotus to world championship. In 1969, he won his fifth Monaco Grand Prix but, after a serious accident, he was subsequently less successful in GP racing, although he won Le Mans 24-hour sports car race in 1972 with Matra.

John Surtees (Great Britain), 1934– Many times world champion racing motorcyclist before taking up car racing in 1961. He was in various teams before joining Ferrari in 1963. He took the world championship with them in 1964 with German and Italian Grands Prix and other high placings.

Surtees stayed with Ferrari two more years but, after a major disagreement, went to Cooper in 1966, winning the Mexican Grand Prix. He raced for Honda in the next two years (winning the Italian Grand Prix), then went to BRM for an unsuccessful 1969 season before forming his own team.

Denny Hulme (New Zealand), 1936– New Zealand Grand Prix Association's 'Driver to Europe' for 1959, but he had several poor years until racing Formula Junior for Brabham, 1963. He became a successful sports car driver, winning the Tourist Trophy 1965/66, and joined Brabham Formula 1 team for 1966.

Hulme won the world championship in 1967, and also had wins at Monaco and in German Grands Prix.

(left) Denny Hulme

(below) John Surtees

He joined McLaren in 1968 and won Can-Am championship as well as Canadian and American Grands Prix. He stayed with McLaren until retiring at the end of 1974, winning a further Can-Am championship, bringing his total of GP wins to eight and Can-Am race wins to 22.

Jackie Stewart (Great Britain), 1939– The driver with most Grand Prix wins to his credit (27) gained between 1965 and 1973, taking the championship three times (1969, 1971 and 1973). He started racing in 1961 and did Formula 3 season for Ken Tyrrell in 1964, being almost unbeatable. He joined BRM in 1965 for single GP wins then and in 1966.

He rejoined Tyrrell with Matra team to gain three GP victories in 1968 and six in 1969. Tyrrell ran his own team in 1970 and they scored one win with a March before producing their own cars in which Stewart scored six GP victories in 1971, four in 1972 and five in 1973.

Jochen Rindt (Austria), 1944–1970 He started racing in 1962 and, by 1964, earned Formula 2 support by Ford Austria. He caused a sensation by beating established stars in British Whitsun F2 meetings and earned Cooper drive for 1965–1967, doing as well as outpaced cars would allow. Dominated 1967 F2 season in Brabham and went to Brabham Formula 1 team for 1968, but his cars were unreliable and he finished only one Grand Prix.

Rindt joined Lotus for 1969 and at last won a Grand Prix. In 1970, he won Monaco, Dutch, French, British and German Grands Prix. He was killed in an Italian GP practice accident but had already earned the world champion title.

Emerson Fittipaldi (Brazil), 1946– He made the most rapid rise to the top in motor racing since

Jackie Stewart   Jochen Rindt

Hawthorn. Brazilian kart and Formula Vee champion. He came to England in 1969 to win both Formula Ford and Formula 3 championships. He joined Lotus Formula 2 team for 1970, and, with Rindt's death, became permanent Formula 1 driver, winning the US Grand Prix.

After an indecisive year in 1971, he won the world championship for Lotus in 1972 with five wins, two seconds and a third. After three more GP wins in 1973 with Lotus, he went to Texaco–Marlboro (McLaren) for 1974, gaining second championship with wins in Brazil, Belgium and Canada.

Ronnie Peterson (Sweden), 1944– Karting and Formula 3 races led to March contract in 1970 with some reasonable successes (including four second places, plus runner-up to Stewart in world championship) in 1971, when he was also European Formula 2 champion.

After some lowly F1 placings with March in 1972 (but several long-distance sports car wins for Ferrari), Peterson moved to Lotus for 1973 and won

(left) Emerson Fittipaldi

(right) Ronnie Peterson

four Grand Prix races, being runner-up to Stewart again. In 1974, he took the Monaco, French and Italian Grands Prix.

Jacky Ickx (Belgium), 1945– After motorcycles and car hillclimbs, he raced Formula 3 for Ken Tyrrell in 1965 and progressed through Formula 2 (Matra) to Formula 1 (Cooper Maserati) before going to Ferrari in 1968, winning the French GP. With Brabham in 1969, he won two Grands Prix, going back to Ferrari and winning three Grands Prix in 1970 and one in each of the following two years, plus many long-distance sports car races.

He joined Lotus for 1974, but his best achievement was in the non-championship Brands Hatch Race of Champions, in the wet, a condition in which he excels.

Jacky Ickx

8: THE ORGANIZATION OF MOTOR SPORT

Motor sport and motor racing in particular, has always been a comparatively orderly affair and, with the knowledge that without order there would be chaos, the majority of participants have agreed readily enough to accept the rules as laid down by mutually accepted authorities.

The first of these authorities, formed in 1895, was the Automobile Club of France, which developed from the committee set up to produce the regulations to govern a major event following the success of the Paris to Rouen trial of 1894. Another early one was the Automobile Club of Great Britain and Ireland, formed in 1897, which in time became the Royal Automobile Club, receiving its patronage from King Edward VII.

Such national bodies eventually came together and the world authority to which nearly all motor sporting organizations ascribe seniority is the *Fédération Internationale de l'Automobile*. Virtually all the national motoring bodies of the world are represented on this. The FIA has many more responsibilities in addition to motor sport and it delegates authority for its sporting activities to the *Commission Sportive Internationale* (CSI); like the FIA, the CSI has its headquarters in Paris.

The CSI effectively governs motor sport although having little contact with the FIA itself. It is also a fully representative body with representatives from all the major sporting nations in the automobile world and quite a few who play a relatively minor role in the world-wide organization. In turn, the CSI delegates its authority to the national automobile clubs of the countries in which motor sport takes place. In the case of Great Britain the ACN (as the national automobile clubs are known) is the Royal Automobile Club.

The RAC is, like the FIA, a body concerned with many other activities apart from motor sport and the sporting side has its own Motor Sport Division, based away from the main part of the RAC. It is run by a professional staff responsible to the RAC and in particular to the British Motor Sport Council. As well as its recognition by the CSI, the Royal Automobile Club carries a responsibility for the Government in that its position is recognized and it takes responsibility for all motoring competitions on the public highway by government decree.

In turn, all officially recognized motor clubs in the country have their sporting activities approved by the RAC and organize them under common regulations. All competitors except those in the most minor events are holders of competition licences issued by the RAC, and all motor racing circuits are licensed by the RAC as are venues for all types of speed events, apart from a very few small competitions such as 'banger' racing which take place mostly without properly organized competition, in farmers' fields, etc.

Motor sport has become a highly political activity during recent years. This is mainly the result of the ever increasing professional involvement. There has been a tendency for each body of people to form themselves into a pressure group to look after their own needs and attempt to bring about a solution to their own particular problems.

Therefore, we have a Formula 1 Constructors' Association made up of the established builders of Grand Prix cars, a Grand Prix Drivers' Association, an International Association of Circuit Owners, a British Circuit Owners Association, a British Trials and Rally Drivers Association and many other smaller bodies, all attempting to do the best they can for their own ends, although it must be said that the majority try, so far as they can manage, to work with other bodies with whom they must deal as amicably as possible. However, there have been many conflicting interests and, on innumerable occasions, there have been pressures brought to change a particular state of affairs; at times the results have not always been in the best interests of all those involved.

Motor Sport Officials and their Responsibilities

The organization of motor sport has become highly developed and virtually all organizers now conform to an established pattern. For example, the various officials of meetings undertake clearly defined responsibilities.

Taking a race meeting as a typical form of motor competition, the senior official at a British meeting is the **RAC Steward**, appointed (as his title implies) by the Royal Automobile Club and having the ultimate responsibility of ensuring that the meeting is run according to the rules laid down by the RAC. The stewards of the meeting have been likened to magistrates of a court and the RAC Steward is the 'Chairman of the Bench'. The other **Stewards** are appointed by the organizing club or clubs, and it is laid down that they are not to be responsible in any way for the organization of the meeting, nor have any executive duty in connection with it. It is the duty of the stewards to adjudicate if any dispute arises between the organizers and competitors, and to deal with the protests, or sit in judgement over a competitor brought before them for a misdemeanour. They have quite wide-ranging powers which permit them to inflict a penalty or a reprimand, to fine or exclude a competitor, to change the course if it is thought necessary, or even amend the results of a competition should they come to the conclusion that a competitor has taken an unfair advantage and the modification is necessary to provide a fair result.

The Clerk of the Course is the chief executive of the meeting on behalf of the organizing club, which is usually a motor club. He has the responsibility for the general running of the meeting and it is up to him to implement the rules as laid down by the controlling body – in the case of competitions within the United Kingdom, the RAC. He ensures that all other officials carry out their duties in the required manner. He controls competitors and their cars, he takes responsibility for the decisions made by the other officials, such as confirming a scrutineer's ruling that a competitor's car is not eligible for an event, or a medical officer who says that a driver is not fit to take part.

It is the Clerk of the Course who is responsible for making sure that the meeting runs to time. He is frequently the starter of each race and it is through him that a competitor is penalized for jumping the start, although such a decision is taken by the judges. He receives protests from competitors and brings them before the stewards. He also takes independent action which may anticipate a protest by deciding that a competitor has acted unfairly and therefore should be penalized, in which case, again, he will bring the competitor before the stewards or perhaps will impose a penalty himself. It is possible that such an action may in itself produce a protest from the competitor penalized.

The Secretary of the Meeting is, as the title implies, the person who collects together all the paper work used in the running of a meeting. It is to him that competitors send in entries. He arranges them into events such as individual races for classes in a race. He collects entry fees. He is also likely to be generally responsible for the production of results (although this may be delegated to others, such as an information officer), and he will probably be responsible for sending out the prizes at the end of the meeting. He may also be responsible for arranging the insurances, obtaining a permit to run the meeting from the controlling body, getting together the material for the programme, compiling and despatching the final instructions for the competitors, etc. In most cases, many of the decisions taken are in consultation with other officials, including the Clerk of the Course.

Judges are appointed where there are decisions to be taken to determine the order of finishing, to decide whether competitors have made a false start, etc. Such officials are judges of fact and, as a rule, their decisions cannot be challenged.

The Chief Medical Officer is normally a doctor who, with one or more other doctors, will be responsible for the medical services at a meeting. No race meeting may take place without at least two doctors being present, together with at least two ambulances, although it is possible for practice to take place with one of each. As well as being responsible for competitors at a race meeting, the Chief Medical Officer also has the responsibility of ensuring that spectators are cared for adequately in an emergency such as a race accident.

All motor racing circuits are required to have a properly established Medical Centre with minimum equipment to ensure that, in an accident, there is a proper place for emergency first-aid and general care to be administered. In addition to doctors there are adequate numbers of first-aid personnel at all motor competitions, and usually more than the required minimum of two ambulances with the personnel to go with them. Doctors at race meetings and other speed events have to be equipped with a minimum standard of apparatus to enable them to cope with likely emergencies.

Circuit medical centres range from simple huts with the minimum amount of equipment laid down to comply with the circuit licence requirements, to miniature hospitals with numerous beds and quite extensive equipment. In addition, the Grand Prix Medical Unit, a mobile 'hospital' provided by charities of a motor racing nature, and containing an X-ray unit, air-conditioned operating theatre and full life support systems, goes to most of the European Grand Prix races, major non-championship Formula 1 events and a number of other leading international meetings, with an attendant staff of specialist operators.

However, the majority of motor racing medical officers take the view that the best way of dealing with motor racing casualties is to provide first-aid, to ensure the sustenance of life and then to remove the injured person as quickly and safely as possible to the nearest suitable hospital with specialist surgeons, for operations and subsequent care. For this reason, the extensive facilities which may be available at race circuits are not always used to the maximum extent.

Scrutineers are the officials who examine the cars taking part in competitions; they have two areas of responsibility. The first is to see that the car is absolutely safe so far as is possible, and there are complex and carefully considered regulations to ensure this safety. The second requirement is to ensure that the cars comply with rules for eligibility, i.e. to make sure that the competitor is not cheating by going outside the rules in an attempt to obtain extra performance. The scrutineering examination will take place prior to the start of the meeting, and in the case of a race meeting, before the car goes out to practise. Scrutineering also continues throughout the meeting to ensure that nothing happens to make a car unsafe, and it will also continue after the meeting to guarantee that the eligibility rules have not been infringed between the first examination and the competition itself.

Timekeepers are the officials who record the performances achieved in a meeting and, like the scrutineers, they are subjected to examinations by the controlling body and are graded according to their ability. They have to equip themselves with watches (chronographs). Timekeepers are allocated within a team so that at most race meetings they are able to record the passage of each and every competitor for every single lap throughout practice and racing. In this way, they provide the times for not only each car as it crosses the finishing line but for every lap achieved by every competitor.

Apart from the permanent staffs employed by the few professional motor racing clubs, scrutineers and timekeepers are normally the only paid officials at any competition, although the RAC Steward receives travelling and other expenses.

Most competitions involve the use of a very substantial number of officials (frequently called marshals) and these are normally headed by a person appointed as **Chief Marshal**. Normally, he is the person responsible for appointing from among known lists of officials, marshals to take part in the general running of the meeting, and at race meetings in particular, to be out on the course.

The **Chief Observer**, usually of equal status to the Chief Marshal, is in general command of the observers and flag marshals at a race meeting. The **Observer** is normally the official in charge of each of the marshals' posts placed strategically round the circuit, one at each corner, and always within sight of the next post in each direction round the course. It is the Observer's duty to note all the occurrences taking place during an incident. He has working under him one or more assistants and several flag marshals as well as fire and course marshals.

Flag marshals are used to inform competitors of various conditions existing during a race – such as when one competitor is trying to overtake another, when there is oil on the track, when there is an obstruction ahead (perhaps a car broken down on the side of the track) or other forms of danger such as a crash, or when there is a course car or ambulance on the track. This is a vital exercise, for there is no other means of communication with the competitor once he is driving on the circuit.

There are many other forms of official such as course marshals who assist with moving broken down cars or ensure that spectators are behind the protective fencing, fire marshals who act as firemen when a car crashes and may burst into flames, paddock marshals who assemble the cars ready for a race, pit marshals who attend and control cars in the pit area of the circuit, startline marshals who assemble the cars on the starting grid and so on.

All these officials have their equivalents in forms of competition other than motor racing. However, they are seldom present in such numbers, with the exception of major rallies, when there is an equivalent number of marshals and control marshals who act as recorders of the progress of the competitors, while there are also emergency services in much the same style as on a race circuit.

Safety Measures in Motor Racing

Through three-quarters of a century of experience, some of it sad, motor sport (and especially racing) has built up a great knowledge of safety requirements. It is an unfortunate reflection upon humanity that these lessons have been ignored continually and, because of this, a most detailed chronicle of requirements has been built up so that, in these days, there is no excuse for inadequate protection of competitors and spectators. The greatly accelerated progress of recent years has resulted in a tremendous improvement in motor racing safety, but only at enormous cost so that, today, the setting up of a circuit to satisfy modern requirements is an exceptionally expensive project.

For the most part, a modern motor racing circuit is encircled by a barrier of steel (in the UK, usually the 'Armco' type) or some other solid vertical wall to contain the cars and prevent them from leaving the extremities of the track. This system is designed to ensure that cars do not get into the spectator areas and it is generally agreed that a vertical barrier minimizes the chances of the driver being badly hurt in an accident. The vertical nature of the barrier will tend to prevent the car from overturning – this being one of the most dangerous hazards to which a racing driver can be subjected.

To reduce the number of heavy impacts from cars running off the track, most motor racing circuits have now been cleared of marshals' posts which could have been hit head-on. These are now normally sited behind the vertical barriers which present a smooth surface to the errant car, at the same time giving greater protection to the marshals themselves.

Posts are linked by telephone (sometimes also by radio) with the Race Control. The usual minimum complement of personnel is an observer, assistant observer and two flag marshals, frequently with additional helpers including course and fire marshals and, at the most dangerous points, doctors.

Unyielding vertical barriers are, of course, highly damaging to the cars and, when struck at a sharp angle, result in an impact which could cause serious injury to a driver even when strapped in. In consequence, efforts have been made to perfect various forms of catch fencing to slow down the car progressively and, if possible, bring it to a standstill before it hits the vertical barrier. Usually, these consist of wire mesh netting mounted on vertical poles which are deliberately weakened at their base; a series of such fences will be positioned before a hazard. A car leaving the circuit will mow down one fence after the other until, hopefully, it is brought to rest without damage of a serious nature to itself and with no hurt to the driver.

Another area of great activity in motor racing safety during recent years has been in fire-fighting, particularly since the death of the Swiss driver, Jo Siffert, at Brands Hatch in 1972. Following this tragedy there was a great outcry against the lack of organization in circuit fire-fighting as it existed at the time. Months of study and practice, during which many systems were tried, resulted in a new form of fire drill which has been standardized at British race circuits and copied widely elsewhere.

This entails positioning groups of four fire marshals at points not more than 200 yards apart all round the track so that the maximum distance they need to move to an emergency is 100 yards. Working as a team, they use two different types of extinguisher – dry powder to 'knock down' the fire and 'light water' (a type of foam) to seal it and prevent re-ignition.

The system is intended to ensure that a fire can be extinguished within 30 seconds of the initial crash – regarded as the time which a driver, wearing the approved type of flame-resistant clothing now used by a large proportion of racing competitors, can be expected to survive in a serious fire. In addition to the groups of four fire marshals at each point, circuits are equipped with fire tenders (usually Land Rovers or similar vehicles), with large capacity extinguishers, acting as a back-up fire-fighting system. However, there is understandable reluctance to mix such relatively slow-moving vehicles with competing cars in the middle of a race before the racing drivers are fully aware of an emergency situation, so the use of fire tenders has to be carried out with caution, to ensure that there is minimal danger of additional incidents.

Race organizations also use 'rescue' vehicles which are usually medium-sized vans equipped with every conceivable item of equipment needed to extinguish fires, remove drivers from smashed vehicles and render first-aid. These are manned by teams of highly trained men, often including a doctor well qualified in casualty work. Besides fire-fighting equipment, the rescue vehicle will normally carry sophisticated hydraulic equipment to force apart crushed bodywork, various forms of cutting tool and medical supplies including resuscitation equipment.

The safety equipment used by drivers is now becoming standardized in nearly all types of car, the exceptions consisting mainly of Vintage and Historic models, which cannot be converted fully to modern requirements without altering their character radically. There is a likelihood that, in time, even these will be converted in an effort to reduce motor racing risks to the lowest level possible for every type of driver.

The most obvious precaution is the wearing of a crash helmet and, for many years now, these have been produced to increasingly high standards to give the best protection possible. Initially they were a development of the type used by motor cyclists, but it was not long before much higher standards were introduced, giving more protection first to the vital temple area of the skull and, more recently, the base of the skull and the jaw area. The modern racing driver wears an all-enveloping helmet which gives him greatly increased protection, but results in his face being entirely invisible to spectators, as he also uses a stone-resistant visor (frequently darkened) over the helmet aperture.

Even if a full-face helmet did not hide the driver's features, he would still be unrecognizable as nowadays the majority wear flame-resistant balaclava helmets as part of their general 'fire proofing'. All professional drivers and a large majority of amateurs also wear perhaps two layers of soft, fire-resistant underwear beneath outer overalls, which are also designed to resist fire. Socks, racing boots and gloves are also of non-flammable materials. The design of this equipment is based on experience gained in the American space exploration field and, although the costs are high, the majority of drivers manage to afford the best clothing in the interests of their own safety.

Compulsory in modern single-seaters and widely used in most other types of car, are full harness safety belts, of aircraft standard webbing. In single-seaters, where the driver lays back in a near-prone position, the harness consists of shoulder, waist and crutch straps, these being joined to a single, quick-release buckle. Where drivers sit more upright, as in saloons, the crutch straps are usually omitted.

The cars themselves are built with cockpits designed to resist deformation in crashes, with roll-over protection hoops above the drivers' heads. Similar protection is fitted into saloons in the form of complete steel roll cages.

In addition to the circuit fire-fighting precautions, competition cars also carry their own fire extinguishers of specified type and size. The more advanced systems have sophisticated arrangements with pipes leading from the extinguisher to critical points around the engine so that, either by a crash-actuated automatic device or by the driver pressing a button, extinguishing fluid or powder is sprayed under pressure into danger areas.

The later type of racing cars have structures that are designed to absorb impacts with a calculated amount of deformation, while leaving the cockpit area undistorted. They also use petrol tanks of rubber-like (but petrol-resistant, of course) flexible bags designed to resist tearing and filled with foam material so that, in the event of rupturing, the leakage of petrol is slow.

A further precaution against fire (usually regarded as the racing driver's worst fear) is for the car to carry an air supply which allows him to breathe in a fire for a short period until he can release himself from the car or until help arrives.

Driver Licensing and Grading

Nowadays, people wishing to take part in motor sport at anything above the lowest level are required to hold competition licences which are used both for registration and as one of the main means of raising funds for the control of motor sport. For example, funds raised by competition licence-fees for British motor sport competitors form a major source of revenue to the controlling body in the UK, the Royal Automobile Club's Motor Sport Division.

The registration of racing and rally drivers has developed into a major safeguard to ensure that incompetent drivers do not hinder the more able ones in competitions and also enables the competitor to learn his sport in relatively mild competition. In the UK, licences are in three categories of Restricted,

National and International, and until the driver has competed regularly and consistently in the lower levels of competition, he cannot obtain a licence for the next level up.

Control is by means of an observation system and the RAC Steward at any race or rally meeting has, as one of his greater responsibilities, the signing of record cards (actually the back of the competitors' licences) indicating that the drivers concerned have competed in a manner above reproach.

Events are also graded into Closed, Restricted (for which a minimum of a Restricted licence is required), National (requiring at least a National licence) and International (requiring full International licences) permit status. Internationals have open or national qualifications, an open one permitting foreign drivers with the appropriate licence to take part.

For all races, competition licence holders must also have a current medical certificate, signed by a qualified doctor, showing that they are medically fit. The examination is a stringent one, covering eyesight, reactions, heart condition, etc.

Additionally, the CSI 'grades' the topmost drivers who may not compete outside their own country, except in the highest level of international competition. This gives a certain amount of exclusiveness to their services but also restricts them by making them ineligible for events other than those in the highest category. The 'graded' drivers are from Grand Prix and long distance (World Championship for Makes) fields and include the world champions from the previous five years and, from the previous two years, those who have figured in the first six of at least two Grand Prix races or, in the case of long distance drivers, those who have finished among the first three pairs.

Drivers' Tuition

Drivers can learn about motor racing by taking professional tuition at recognized racing schools. In North America, a compulsory system of training is enforced, organized by the Sports Car Club of America.

In Europe, attendance at racing drivers' schools is voluntary but becoming more widely accepted as the quickest and most efficient way of learning how to drive successfully at racing speeds. A typical racing school (e.g. Motor Racing Stables at Brands Hatch) gives the would-be pupil a trial run in a saloon car, with an instructor beside him, to assess his ability. Those found capable are then given a short run of several laps in a single-seater to give them an idea of what is involved. From then on, a detailed course in racing technique is followed by private races, restricted to school pupils and using school cars. By the conclusion of the course the pupil will have had a substantial experience of actual racing, as well as tuition concerning the finer points of the sport.

Timekeepers and Timekeeping

While it may seem simple in an event like a motor race to decide who has actually won, this may not be as obvious as it seems. A system must be established to record the competitors who hold the lead throughout the race and a calculation must be made to issue the winner's speed, for comparison with other races.

It does not take much development of this theme to require a whole team of timekeepers for each race meeting. These are among the busiest and most highly qualified of the race officials. Timekeepers are graded according to their ability and experience, and they are required to equip themselves with extremely accurate (and expensive) stopwatches –

known officially as chronographs – which are certified by appropriate authorities such as the National Physical Laboratory. A top grade timekeeper will be able to record, accurately, the passage of four to five cars, each passing him once every 45 seconds or so, for perhaps 30 laps of a race. In doing so he will note the car number, number of laps completed, running time and individual lap time of each and every competitor for which he is responsible. Accordingly, immediately after the field has passed the finishing flag, he can provide all the relevant information so that a complete result, with fastest laps in each class (or even of every competitor) can be written out without delay.

As an alternative to stopwatches, timing may be by automatic equipment (usually by the competing car breaking a light beam), which prints out the time on a sheet of paper. The numbers of the cars are recorded as they cross the line and are related to the printed times; the timekeepers are then organized into a team to extract the information and interpret it for the production of results.

9: WORLD RACING CIRCUITS

BARCELONA, Spain
2.35 miles, 3.78 km

BRANDS HATCH, Kent, England

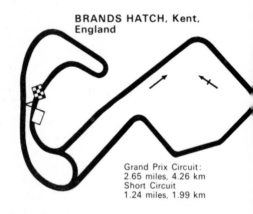

Grand Prix Circuit:
2.65 miles, 4.26 km
Short Circuit
1.24 miles, 1.99 km

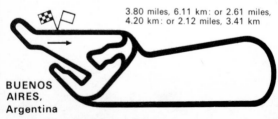

3.80 miles, 6.11 km: or 2.61 miles,
4.20 km: or 2.12 miles, 3.41 km

BUENOS AIRES, Argentina

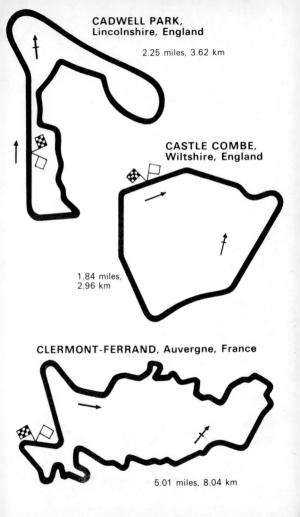

CADWELL PARK,
Lincolnshire, England

2.25 miles, 3.62 km

CASTLE COMBE,
Wiltshire, England

1.84 miles,
2.96 km

CLERMONT-FERRAND, Auvergne, France

5.01 miles, 8.04 km

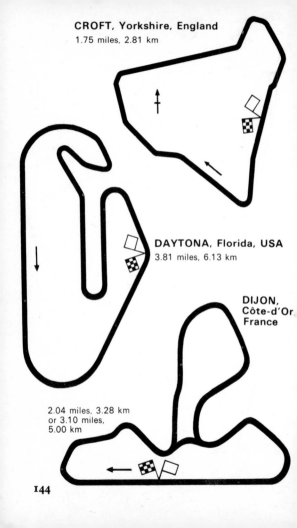

CROFT, Yorkshire, England
1.75 miles, 2.81 km

DAYTONA, Florida, USA
3.81 miles, 6.13 km

DIJON, Côte-d'Or France

2.04 miles, 3.28 km
or 3.10 miles, 5.00 km

144

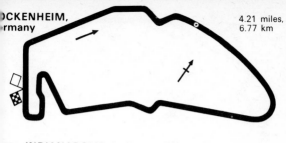

HOCKENHEIM, Germany

4.21 miles, 6.77 km

INDIANAPOLIS, Indiana, USA

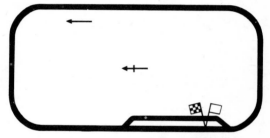

2.5 miles, 4.02 km

INGLISTON, Midlothian, Scotland

1.03 miles, 1.65 km

**INTERLAGOS,
São Paulo,
Brazil**

4.94 miles, 7.95 km

JARAMA, Madrid, Spain
2.11 miles, 3.39 km

**KYALAMI, Johannesburg,
South Africa**

2.55 miles, 4.10 km

146

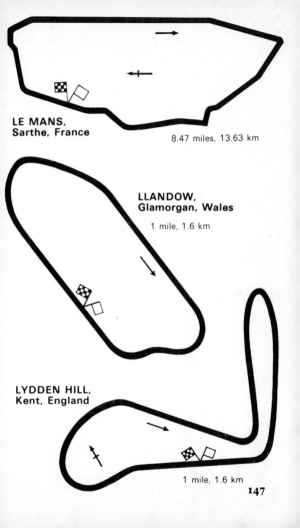

LE MANS,
Sarthe, France

8.47 miles, 13.63 km

LLANDOW,
Glamorgan, Wales

1 mile, 1.6 km

LYDDEN HILL,
Kent, England

1 mile, 1.6 km

MALLORY PARK, Leicestershire, England

1.35 miles, 2.17 km: or 1 mile, 1.6 km

MONACO

2.03 miles, 3.26 km

**MONDELLO PARK,
Near Dublin, Ireland**

1.24 miles,
1.99 km

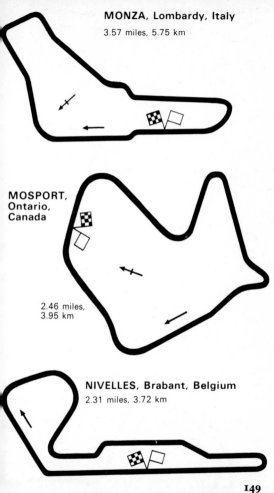

MONZA, Lombardy, Italy

3.57 miles, 5.75 km

MOSPORT,
Ontario,
Canada

2.46 miles,
3.95 km

NIVELLES, Brabant, Belgium

2.31 miles, 3.72 km

NÜRBURGRING,
West Germany

14.18 miles, 22.83 km

OSTERREICHRING,
Austria

3.67 miles, 5.91 km

OULTON PARK,
Cheshire,
England

2.76 miles, 4.44 km:
or 1.65 miles,
2.66 km

PAUL RICARD, Provence, France

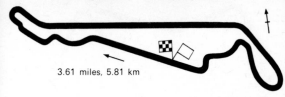

3.61 miles, 5.81 km

PHOENIX PARK, Dublin, Ireland

2.77 miles, 4.45 km

SANDOWN, Melbourne, Australia

1.93 miles, 3.10 km

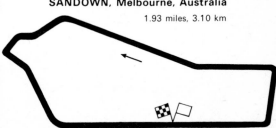

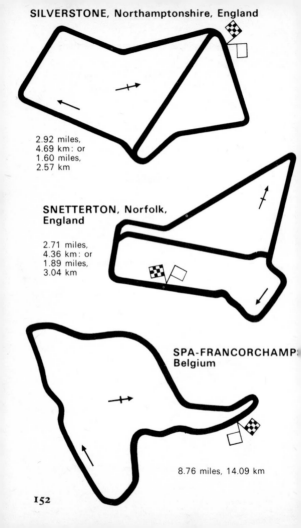

SILVERSTONE, Northamptonshire, England

2.92 miles,
4.69 km: or
1.60 miles,
2.57 km

**SNETTERTON, Norfolk,
England**

2.71 miles,
4.36 km: or
1.89 miles,
3.04 km

SPA-FRANCORCHAMP
Belgium

8.76 miles, 14.09 km

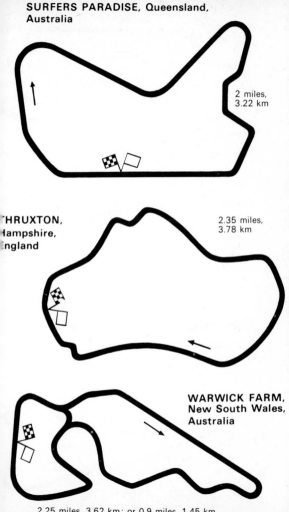

SURFERS PARADISE, Queensland, Australia

2 miles, 3.22 km

THRUXTON, Hampshire, England

2.35 miles, 3.78 km

WARWICK FARM, New South Wales, Australia

2.25 miles, 3.62 km: or 0.9 miles, 1.45 km

WATKINS GLEN, New York State, USA

3.37 miles, 5.42 km

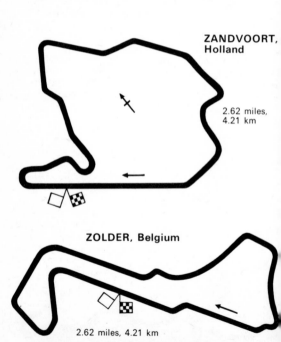

ZANDVOORT, Holland

2.62 miles, 4.21 km

ZOLDER, Belgium

2.62 miles, 4.21 km

10: WORLD CHAMPIONSHIP OF DRIVERS, 1950-75

It is perhaps somewhat surprising that there was no world championship for drivers before 1950 because motor racing was rather more highly organized in the years immediately prior to World War II than it was in the period shortly after it. Even so, there had been no world championship before the war. There had, however, been a European championship, which, in the 1930s, was dominated by the drivers of the Mercedes-Benz and Auto-Union cars.

When motor racing resumed after World War II, the Grand Prix formula was based on the voiturette formula of the pre-war days, being basically for cars up to $1\frac{1}{2}$-litres supercharged but with the additional provision for cars of up to $4\frac{1}{2}$-litres unsupercharged.

When Alfa Romeo decided to take part in Grand Prix racing they were completely in command with the pre-war Type 158 car (subsequently developed and called 159), which was immeasurably superior to its rivals.

In 1950 there were six European races counting towards the championship and all were won by Alfa Romeo, with three races going to the Italian, Giuseppe Farina, and the other three going to the Argentinian, Juan Manuel Fangio. Farina, as a result of some higher placings in the races that he did not win, was the first world champion driver with 30 points, Fangio was second with 27 points while another Italian, Luigi Fagioli, also driving for Alfa Romeo, was third with 24.

The 1951 season was very much more competitive. The Ferrari team switched from their supercharged $1\frac{1}{2}$-litre car to one with a $4\frac{1}{2}$-litre unsupercharged engine. It took some time to become both fast and reliable but, at the British Grand Prix at Silverstone, Fangio's compatriot, Jose Froilan Gonzales, out-drove him to break the Alfa Romeo domination.

Alberto Ascari, son of one of the great drivers of the 1920s, followed up Gonzales's Silverstone success for Ferrari by winning both the German Grand Prix at the Nürburgring and the Italian Grand Prix at Monza.

Alfa Romeo still won the championship through Fangio, who scored 31 points by winning the Swiss and Spanish Grands Prix as well as sharing the French Grand Prix with Fagioli, but Ascari was runner-up with 25 points, while Gonzales was third with 22.

It was clear to Alfa Romeo that their great 'Alfetta' (as the Type 158/159 was known) had reached the end of the development road and there was no prospect of challenging the Ferrari in 1952. In consequence, Alfa Romeo announced its withdrawal from Grand Prix racing, leaving Ferrari without effective competition.

The powers that be decided to drop the $1\frac{1}{2}$-litre supercharged/$4\frac{1}{2}$-litre unsupercharged Formula 1 for the Grand Prix seasons of 1952 and 1953, which were to be the last two of that formula. Instead it was decided to run the world championship for Formula 2 cars which were 2-litre unsupercharged models. If this was intended to prevent a Ferrari walk-over, then the formula change was a complete failure! In 1952, Ferrari won each of the seven rounds of the championship with Ascari taking all but one victory, which went to his compatriot and team-mate Piero Taruffi in the Swiss Grand Prix.

In 1953, there were eight rounds of the championship and of these Ascari won five. The British driver, Mike Hawthorn, and Farina won a race each, also for Ferrari, while the exception was Fangio who won the Italian Grand Prix at Monza for Maserati.

In fact, 1953 was a very much more competitive year with the Maseratis closer to the Ferraris in performance. Fangio was unlucky not to win the French Grand Prix on the Rheims-Gueux circuit in what has become regarded as one of the classic motor races of all time, with Fangio and Hawthorn passing and re-passing all round the track on lap after lap. Hawthorn, who was in his first season with a major Grand Prix team and had started motor racing only two years previously, won the race by out-smarting Fangio on acceleration from the final corner. Ascari won the world championship for the second time, but Fangio was runner-up with Farina in third place.

The new formula for 1954, for unsupercharged cars up to $2\frac{1}{2}$-litres, opened the most competitive era of Grand Prix racing for many years, and for the first time, the title of 'World' Championship was justified.

Fangio now assumed a dominant role and displayed his almost uncanny ability to choose the most successful team. For 1954 he signed up to drive a new Mercedes-Benz but, as this was not to be ready until the middle of the season, he began with the new Maserati 250F and won at the Argentine Grand Prix at Buenos Aires and at the Belgian Grand Prix on the extremely fast Spa-Francorchamps circuit.

In time for the French Grand Prix at Rheims, the new Mercedes-Benz W196 was ready in its initial streamlined form and, backed up by Karl Kling, Fangio duly won on this circuit which was highly suited to the streamlined car. The car was less impressive at the British Grand Prix at Silverstone where its handling did not suit the circuit conditions, Fangio hitting oil drums used for marking the corners. The race was won by Gonzales (Ferrari) with Fangio and his badly-battered Mercedes well behind.

Within weeks, a revised model appeared for the German Grand Prix at the Nürburgring with unenclosed wheels and more conventional bodywork. Here Fangio proved to be unbeatable, as in the subsequent Swiss and Italian Grands Prix, taking his second world championship.

For 1955, Fangio and Kling were joined by Stirling Moss, who soon took on the mantle of Fangio's shadow. Their cars were clearly superior to the opposition and usually very reliable, although they expired at Monaco, leaving the Frenchman, Maurice Trintignant, to win in a Ferrari. However, the Maserati 250F was still going extremely well and there were new rivals appearing such as the Vanwall and Connaught from Great Britain, not to mention a new 4-cylinder BRM, Gordinis and, later on, even a Bugatti from France.

Fangio won the Argentine, Belgian, Dutch and Italian Grands Prix all for Mercedes-Benz, and Moss won the British Grand Prix at Aintree to become the first British driver to win a round of the world championship.

Having won the championship so convincingly, Mercedes-Benz withdrew at the end of 1955. Fangio chose Ferrari for 1956 and Moss went to Maserati. Both enjoyed successful seasons, Fangio winning his home (Argentine) Grand Prix for the third successive year, the British Grand Prix at Silverstone and the German Grand Prix at the Nürburgring, to clinch his third successive world championship, while Moss won the Monaco and Italian

Grands Prix for Maserati. The young British driver, Peter Collins, Fangio's Ferrari team-mate, won the Belgian and French Grands Prix.

Significant non-championship races of this period were the 1955 Syracuse Grand Prix in Sicily, which was won by the then unknown British driver Tony Brooks in a completely new Connaught, and the 1956 International Trophy race at Silverstone which was won by Moss in a new Vanwall.

For 1957 and 1958 there was a general shuffle round of the leading drivers with Moss going to the Vanwall team together with Brooks (who had spent a frustrating 1956 with Hawthorn in the BRM team). Hawthorn went back to the Ferrari team to join his great friend Peter Collins, while Fangio decided that the Maserati 250F was the best bet.

Fangio demonstrated that, for 1957 at least, he had made a wise choice by winning the Argentine, Monaco and French Grands Prix, but he and the Maserati were nearing the end of the road of success. At the 1957 British Grand Prix at Aintree, Moss again created history, this time by bringing home a British car to win the British Grand Prix, taking over the Vanwall of Tony Brooks when his own car had fuel injection troubles. From that point on, British Grand Prix motor racing was in the ascendant and Moss won subsequent races for Vanwall in Italy where, that year, there were two championship races at Pescara and Monza. However, Fangio and the Maserati were not quite finished and, in a race of tactics at the Nürburgring, Fangio decided to start on a partially empty tank to improve his car's weight distribution and handling, although well aware that this would entail a pit stop. As expected, he led until then, restarting well behind Hawthorn and Collins in their Ferraris. Smashing the course record lap after lap, Fangio pulled in the two young drivers in one of the several legendary drives of his career to win his fourth Grand Prix of the season, which was also the 24th and last of his great career (clinching his fifth world championship), plus the final Grand Prix success of the Maserati.

From 1958 there was a significant change in the formula. Cars had to be run on petrol. In particular, the Vanwall, Ferrari and Coventry Climax engines ran without noticeable difficulties on the 'new' fuel. The Vanwall team did not go to the Argentine Grand Prix and, instead, Moss chose to drive the little Cooper (at that stage with a 2-litre Coventry Climax engine) for the private entrant Rob Walker. This little car pulled off the first Grand Prix success by a rear-engined model since the days of the Auto-Union, but the effort was regarded as a mere flash in the pan. Generally it was still disregarded when the same car won the Monaco Grand Prix in the hands of Maurice Trintignant, after the exuberant young favourites such as Moss, Collins and Hawthorn all crashed in the same incident in the early stages of the race.

Although significant, these Cooper successes resulted from the car's suitability to tight circuits, which gave it a special advantage. The main battle of the season was between Ferrari and Vanwall with Hawthorn, backed up by Collins and the American Phil Hill, against the Vanwalls of Moss, Brooks and Stuart Lewis-Evans.

Hawthorn won only a single race (the French Grand Prix) as did Collins (the British Grand Prix), while Moss – in addition to his Argentine Grand Prix win in the Cooper – won the Dutch, Portuguese and Moroccan Grands Prix, and Brooks won the Belgian, German and Italian events. However, such was Hawthorn's consistency in picking up second places that he ran out champion with 42 points to Moss's 41. It was the fourth year in a row that Moss was second in the championship.

Because of the ill-health of its patron, Tony Vandervell, the Vanwall team withdrew at the end of the 1958 season, having won the manufacturers' championship conclusively – this being the first year of this extra world championship competition. Hawthorn retired at the end of the season, saddened by the death of his great friend, Collins, in a crash that he witnessed. He did not live long to enjoy being the first British champion, dying in a road accident within months.

The change-round in 1959 saw Brooks as No. 1 for Ferrari and Moss in Rob Walker's privately entered Cooper.

Much more notice was now taken of the rear-engined Cooper design and it was Jack Brabham of Australia in the works Cooper who became champion with wins at Monaco and the British Grand Prix at Aintree. A win by New Zealander Bruce McLaren in the American Grand Prix clinched the manufacturers' championship for Cooper even without Moss's wins in Portugal and Italy. Brooks won in France and Germany to take second place in the championship, while Moss was third. BRM had their first-ever world championship win that year when Joakim Bonnier of Sweden won the Dutch Grand Prix for the hitherto unsuccessful British team. It was the first and only Grand Prix win for a front-engined BRM.

The final year of the $2\frac{1}{2}$-litre formula confirmed the supremacy of the rear-engined design with Brabham and Cooper taking the championships for the second successive year, Brabham scoring five wins in Holland, Belgium, France, Great Britain and Portugal. Moss, again driving for Rob Walker's private team, gave the Lotus its first Grand Prix victories at Monaco and in the United States. Phil Hill managed a single win for Ferrari with the final victory for a front-engined car at the Italian Grand Prix.

In the dying days of the $2\frac{1}{2}$-litre formula, the British contestants tried to forestall the proposed $1\frac{1}{2}$-litre formula which was to follow, by threatening to boycott, while making inadequate preparations to cope with the change.

Ferrari quietly got on with the job of building a competitive car for the $1\frac{1}{2}$-litre formula, but the British contestants had to make do with the old (previously Formula 2) $1\frac{1}{2}$-litre 4-cylinder Coventry Climax FPF engine – the fore-runner of the $2\frac{1}{2}$-litre unit which had been the most successful engine of the previous two seasons.

Only the brilliant driving of Moss in the Rob Walker Lotus was any match for the V6 Ferraris and then only at the right sort of circuit, where his driving ability could overcome the disparity in power output. Moss won at Monte Carlo and the Nürburgring to bring to a close his brilliant career as a Grand Prix driver (he had a serious accident at Goodwood the following Easter) while Ferrari won elsewhere, although, again, the championship victory was marred by tragedy as the champion-elect, German driver Wolfgang von Trips, was killed at Monza in a collision with Jim Clark's Lotus. Von Trips had won the Dutch and British Grands Prix. Instead the championship went to his team-mate Phil Hill, who had already won at the Belgian Grand Prix and was to be the winner at Monza

In Ferrari's absence, the Lotus works team won their first Grand Prix when Innes Ireland won in the USA.

At the German Grand Prix, Jack Brabham (as the reigning world champion) was entrusted with the first $1\frac{1}{2}$-litre V8 Coventry Climax FWMV engine in his works Cooper, but an off-course excursion made the project inconclusive.

However, the following season the British V8-engined cars proved supreme and the season was a tremendous battle between the Lotus Climax of Jim Clark and BRM using their own V8 engine, with Graham Hill as the leading driver. After so many years with scant success, it was to be a make or break year for BRM, whose patron, Sir Alfred Owen, made it clear to the team that they must win two Grands Prix or be disbanded. In fact, Hill was to win four Grands Prix with successes in Holland, Germany, Italy and South Africa. Clark also started his Grand Prix successes which were to continue until he created a record, eventually winning 25 Grands Prix (one more than Fangio). In 1962 Clark won in Belgium, Great Britain, and the United States and he was actually leading the final (South African) race when his car broke down, giving the championship to Hill.

Despite its initial unpopularity, the $1\frac{1}{2}$-litre formula was proving to be immensely competitive and cars were no slower than they had been in the previous $2\frac{1}{2}$-litre era, thanks to superior road-holding and the not inconsiderable power of the more sophisticated 8-cylinder engines. The BRM was still competitive in 1963 and Hill started the season with the first of three successive Monaco Grand Prix wins for the marque, following this up by winning the United States Grand Prix. Clark was in tremendous form with the monocoque Lotus 25 car and for 1963 the Coventry Climax engine was fitted with fuel injection which made it even more powerful. Clark won no fewer than seven Grands Prix – a record.

Although overshadowed in the two previous seasons, Ferrari was still very much in the reckoning and took the 1964 Championship through the efforts of John Surtees, previously one of the greatest motorcycle riders of all time. He had won the 1963 German Grand Prix for Ferrari and was to repeat this success in 1964 as well as taking the Italian Grand Prix. He was well-placed consistently so that he scored 40 points to the 39 of Hill's BRM, with two Grand Prix wins. Despite three wins, Clark was only third with 32 points. This season also saw the first major success for Brabham's new team, although the two Grand Prix victories came as the result of the driving of American Dan Gurney and not through Brabham himself.

The 1965 season was the last one for the $1\frac{1}{2}$-litre formula and again was dominated by Clark in a Lotus with six Grand Prix wins, gaining 54 points to Graham Hill's 40. Third place in the championship was taken by Jackie Stewart who began his career as the most successful Grand Prix driver of all time. He scored 33 points with a BRM, although he won only a single Grand Prix – the Italian event.

The new formula for 1966 was for cars with unsupercharged engines up to 3,000 cc. In spite of ample warning, most teams were caught without a suitable engine and it was Jack Brabham who created history by becoming the first world champion in a car of his own make. He used the relatively simple Australian Repco engine which was not particularly powerful but was reliable and light. The highly roadworthy Brabham-Tauranac chassis, with Brabham's undoubted ability as a driver, resulted in his winning four times in the French, British, Dutch and German Grands Prix.

The Ferrari 312 was potentially a world-beater and Surtees gave it a win at the Belgian Grand Prix on the fast Spa circuit, but midway through the season he had a great argument with the team management and left to join Cooper. He drove the unwieldy

Maserati-powered cars for the rest of the year, securing a win in the Mexican Grand Prix to give himself second place in the championship over his Cooper team-mate, the Austrian Jochen Rindt. BRM were striving to win with another complicated engine design – an H16 – but their only success came as a result of using the earlier V8, bored out to 2 litres, on the twisty Monaco circuit. Lotus (with similar engine problems) also used the H16 BRM unit and with this Clark won the final race of the season, the United States Grand Prix at Watkins Glen.

The 1967 season started with the Brabham team again the one to beat and their successes included two victories for Brabham himself and two more for the New Zealander Denny Hulme, who won at Monaco and the Nürburgring (the two great 'drivers'' circuits). This gave Hulme the championship but the really significant event of the season was the arrival of the V8 Ford-Cosworth DFV engine for the Lotus team which now included both Clark and Hill. Clark followed a first-time-out win at the Dutch Grand Prix with more victories in the British, United States and Mexican Grands Prix in the Lotus 49 car.

Otherwise, 12-cylinder engines were becoming popular with wins for the Japanese Honda (Surtees driving), Cooper-Maserati (Pedro Rodriguez) and Eagle – a new make powered by a British Weslake engine and built by Dan Gurney, who drove it to victory in the Belgian Grand Prix.

The 1968 season saw the emergence of yet another team led by a driver building his own cars, Bruce McLaren. He was joined by the reigning champion, Denny Hulme, who won the Canadian Grand Prix, while McLaren himself joined the ranks of those drivers who won Grand Prix races in cars of their own make, with a victory in the

Belgian Grand Prix. For 1968, Cosworth-Ford V8 engines were available not only to Lotus but to anyone who could afford the £7,000 purchase price.

Ferrari re-entered the victors' ranks with a new version of the 312, driven by the Belgian Jacky Ickx in the French Grand Prix. He won with a car employing 'wings'—aerodynamic downthrust devices to give extra loading onto the wheels, to keep them in firmer contact with the ground and therefore creating greater cornering power. Immediately, every team took to using 'wings', including many weird and fragile systems.

Earlier in the season, Lotus had suffered the terrible blow of losing Jim Clark, who was killed in a Formula 2 race in Germany, having already demonstrated his winning form by taking the South African Grand Prix at the beginning of the season. Hill gave the team its third world championship with wins in the Spanish, Monaco and Mexican Grands Prix, while yet another major team emerged in Matra, using the Ford V8 engine and managed by Ken Tyrrell, who had Jackie Stewart as his No. 1 driver. This team secured wins in the Dutch, German and United States Grands Prix, so that Stewart was a runner-up to Hill in the World Championship, with Hulme in third place.

In 1969 there was no holding the Matra-Ford team and Stewart scored six wins in the season. At Monaco, Hill earned the distinction of scoring his fifth Grand Prix on that circuit. After four years of trying in the Cooper, Brabham and Lotus teams, Jochen Rindt finally won a Grand Prix at the end of the 1969 season – the United States Grand Prix.

Rindt continued winning during 1970 with the new Lotus 72 car although he started the season with a somewhat lucky win at the Monaco Grand Prix in the earlier Type 49. Once the 72 had become fully competitive at the Dutch Grand Prix he was very difficult to beat and won that race together with the French, British and German events. Unfortunately he was killed while practising for the Italian Grand Prix at Monza. Rindt became the first driver to be awarded the world championship posthumously. Lotus secured the Manufacturers' Championship as a result of a win in the final race of the year in America by Emerson Fittipaldi of Brazil, whose rise to fame was quicker than anybody's since the days of Mike Hawthorn, as he had been driving in Formula Ford only the previous season.

But for Fittipaldi's success, the Manufacturers' Championship could have gone to Ferrari for whom Ickx scored three wins and the Swiss, Clay Regazzoni, one. 1970 also saw the appearance of two new makes of car, the March (in which Stewart won the Spanish Grand Prix early in the year) and the Tyrrell. Ken Tyrrell decided to construct his own car when Matra withdrew their chassis from him because the French team wanted to use their own V12 engine, while Tyrrell and Stewart preferred the Ford. The Tyrrell car was already proving competitive towards the end of the 1970 season.

BRM had their best season for several years with Pedro Rodriguez winning the Belgian Grand Prix and nearly winning the United States Grand Prix as well.

After its promise at the end of the 1970 season, the Tyrrell was the car to beat during 1971, although the season started with a win for Ferrari by the American Mario Andretti in South Africa. Then Stewart recorded his series of six wins for Tyrrell to clinch his second championship. Ickx scored for Ferrari at the Dutch Grand Prix, Jo Siffert of Switzerland and Peter Gethin (Great Britain) won for BRM in Austria and Italy, while François Cevert of France won the final race for Tyrrell, to

167

come third in the championship. Yet the runner-up was Ronnie Peterson of Sweden in the March 711. He did not win a single Grand Prix, but he finished second on no fewer than four occasions and had other high placings.

Some promising performances were achieved by Emerson Fittipaldi during the 1971 season including second places in South Africa and Austria, and he became the youngest-ever world champion in 1972 when the Lotus 72 car (now running as the John Player Special) proved more successful than any other. Fittipaldi won five GPs to the four of Stewart in the Tyrrell.

The pace hotted up even further in 1973 when Jackie Stewart, with five more victories, took his third championship and became the driver to score more world championship wins than any other before him (27 in all), but the Tyrrell was hounded all the way by the Lotus 72/John Player Specials of Emerson Fittipaldi and Ronnie Peterson, who between them won seven rounds.

At the end of 1973, Stewart announced his retirement and left the stage clear for 1974. This was to be the most competitive year ever in the history of Grand Prix racing, although it has also been argued that the situation was created by Stewart's departure, which left Grand Prix racing without a top class driver according to his standards.

Be that as it may, by the seventh race of the 1974 series, there had been six different winners, these being Denny Hulme (Texaco Marlboro McLaren) and his team-mate Emerson Fittipaldi (the only driver who had won twice at that stage), Carlos Reutemann of Argentina (Brabham), Niki Lauda of Austria (Ferrari), Ronnie Peterson (John Player Special) and the young South African Jody Scheckter (Elf-Tyrrell).

By the 11th race, the German Grand Prix, Clay

Regazzoni (Ferrari) had also won, having led the championship for much of the year through consistently high placings. With only two races to go, there were still five drivers in a position to win the championship, these being Regazzoni, Scheckter, Fittipaldi, Lauda and Peterson, and it was not until the final round, the US Grand Prix, that there were 'only' three contenders – Fittipaldi and Regazzoni with equal points, and Scheckter, who finished in that order, with 55, 52 and 45 points respectively. The next three were Lauda (38), Peterson (35) and Reutemann (32). Fittipaldi, Peterson and Reutemann all had three victories each while Scheckter and Lauda both had two.

The Ford-Cosworth engine chalked up its 100th victory during the season and it was notable that 10 different makes scored championship points during the season, of which all but Ferrari and BRM used the Ford V8 unit.

The 1975 season began in similar fashion to the previous year, with each of the first four races won by a different driver (Emerson Fittipaldi and Carlos Pace appropriately in the South American events and Jody Scheckter equally so in South Africa), although Jochen Mass scored only half points in Spain. This was because the race was stopped before half distance when Rolf Stommelen's car crashed into a marshals' compound, killing four people.

From then on, however, the races were largely dominated by the Ferrari of Niki Lauda of Austria, who achieved pole positions in practice for most of the year's events and won three Grands Prix (Monaco, Belgium and Sweden) in succession.

Lauda clinched the championship finally at the Italian Grand Prix which ended the European part of the championship year.

11: OTHER FORMS OF MOTOR SPORT

Rallies

As a sporting activity, motor rallies are as old as racing and, these days, even more popular. The name implies a getting-together of people with motor cars, but it was very long ago that the sport developed greatly beyond that situation. Indeed, in the average rally, about the last thing that competitors do is to gather together and, in contrast to racing, they spend most of their time running entirely on their own.

The rally is the obvious extension of the very early reliability trials and soon developed into a contest to decide which sorts of car and which drivers were superior to their rivals.

In the early days it was an achievement just to finish the course without breaking down and give reasonable performances on the hillclimbs and other tests which existed on the route. As time went on, and cars became more efficient, it became necessary to make the events progressively tougher and more ambitious.

Those who think that the London–Sydney Marathon of 1967 and the World Cup Rally of 1970 were long and difficult events should remember that as early as 1907 there was a Paris to Peking trial held under infinitely more difficult circumstances.

Perhaps the classic rally (although it has been largely discredited in recent years, through the uncompromising attitude of the organizers) is the Monte Carlo Rally which became the world's leading non-racing event in the days before the war and reached a new peak of popularity in the 1950s and 1960s.

In its early days, it was a rally as the word implies, with starting-points in various parts of Europe and a long trek over difficult roads to join up, usually in the north of France, and then the whole entry would travel together to the Principality of Monaco. It was expected that, by the time that the entry had reached the town of Monte Carlo, competitors would have lost enough points to produce a result. When the cars and their crews became more efficient, extra tests at Monte Carlo were used to determine the finishing positions, such as driving tests and even races round the well-known Grand Prix circuit. In later years, the modern Monte Carlo Rally has included 'special stages' in the mountains behind the principality which are, effectively, races against the clock over ice-bound passes where incredible deeds of daring are required to become one of the winners.

At the other end of the scale there have been huge numbers of smaller rallies in all parts of the world which are typified today by the 12-car events run by small motor clubs throughout the United Kingdom. In between these two extremes, there are a great variety of rallies of all types of which the American sort of event is dependent largely on excesses of accurate time-keeping and regularity while, in under-developed countries, the event is more of a car-breaking race where the winners are those who can get nearest to the impossible time schedules set by the organizers.

Now generally regarded as one of the best and most difficult rallies is the RAC Rally of Great Britain which, in recent years, has been developed to a high pitch of efficiency in providing a tremendous test for both man and machine, whilst retaining a great degree of popularity with the competitors who are likely to number something in excess of 300 cars with their crews. The basis of the event is a fairly simple and undemanding route between a large number of special stages, these tests being many types of road or rough track section for which a bogey time is set, generally requiring a speed which is above that which the organizers expect even the fastest competitor to achieve. Accordingly, the number of points lost by competitors show very clearly those entries which are superior for the event, which demands the utmost in performance, controllability and reliability from the cars and skill and tenacity on the part of the crews.

The majority of successful rally drivers at the present time are Scandinavian in origin and it has been found that these Swedes and Finns are superlative at controlling their cars over surfaces lacking in adhesion such as ice, loose stones and rutted track. However, there are still British, French, Italian and German drivers who can rival the northerners, and the level of competition to achieve success in many rallies is intense.

Except for the recent expansion in production saloon car racing, nothing has attracted the support of motor manufacturers in competition so much as rallies in which the majority of car manufacturers all over the world have either entered teams directly or given extensive background support to private entrants. This support has proved that their products are suitable for this form of competition which appeals to the ordinary motorist as something for which his own car is fully suited.

The immense crowds of spectators who have swarmed to the special stages on the RAC Rally in recent years have brought claims that this is by far the most highly attended sporting event in the country and suggest that the ordinary man in the street is very much more interested in motor sport

The Ford Escort is possibly the most successful competition car ever built. Here Hannu Mikkola wins the East African Safari rally

than is generally realized, providing that he can relate it to the sort of car which he drives himself. From the manufacturers' point of view, there is certainly a very rapid feed-back in information on what cars will achieve or otherwise in rallies than in most other forms of motor sport.

Rallies such as the 1,000-Lakes event in Finland, the Midnight Sun in Sweden, the Acropolis Rally in Greece, the Press-on-Regardless in Canada and (probably the greatest of them all) the East African Safari, all attract big entries from the major contestants and are both demanding and rewarding to the competitors and the manufacturers whom they represent.

There is almost no end to the variety which rallies can take and they can be used in many different ways to test and prove the various qualities of the motor car. With fuel conservation as a great problem at the present time, it is likely that there will be an increase in events such as the Total Economy Drive (successor to the well-known Mobil

Economy Run) in which competitors are expected to achieve remarkable fuel consumption figures over difficult courses under strict observation to prevent coasting, while maintaining set average speeds. Performances such as 60 miles (96 km) per gallon in 1,000 cc cars are the targets at which competitors aim. The growing demand to relate competition motoring to ordinary production cars is likely to see an extension of rallies like the Avon Motor Tour of Britain, which is a mixture of races and rally special stages for purely standard cars and has been seized upon as a challenge between racing drivers and rally drivers.

In their highest form, rallies are very expensive events demanding extreme levels of organization and the support of highly trained service crews, while the competitors may spend weeks or even months carrying out reconnaissances of the route. Other events specifically ban such reconnaissances or the use of pace notes (notes which can be used to warn the driver of the road hazards ahead and which indicate the speed with which corners may be taken safely) or even the use of service crews in support of competing cars.

After a lifetime of trials and rallying in which there was no particular nation whose drivers could be regarded as supreme in this branch of motor sport, the men of Scandinavia, more specifically of Sweden and Finland, emerged as a breed of super-drivers who have almost dominated rallying for much of the sixties and seventies.

There is good reason for the way in which the Scandinavians have proved most successful in rallying. The nature of modern rallies has altered so that the more difficult and challenging parts now take place under just the conditions of snow and ice, or loose surfaces similar to the partially made-up roads generally found north of the Arctic Circle in the summer months, which these drivers have come to regard as normal since their first days at the wheel of a car.

Eric Carlsson of Sweden was the first to make a major impact, driving the Saab cars whose performance in his hands belied the small size (up to 850 cc) of their two-stroke engines.

Among the first to appreciate fully the inherent ability of these Scandinavian rally drivers was Stuart Turner, motoring journalist turned competitions manager of the British Motor Corporation. He used them more and more in his team, a process he continued later with even greater success when he became Ford of Britain's director of competitions.

Under Turner's direction, Timo Makinen of Finland performed wonders with the Mini-Cooper and, much later, with Ford Escorts. Even more successful was another Finn, Hannu Mikkola, who won for Ford the World Cup Rally of 1970. This event began at Wembley Stadium in London, scene of British football's triumph in the 1966 World Cup competition, and ended in Mexico City, venue of the 1970 Cup, running first through Europe and then going almost the entire length of South and Central America.

Later, in 1972, accompanied once more by the Swedish co-driver Gunnar Palm (who shared with him the World Cup success), Mikkola became the first driver not resident in East Africa to win the Safari Rally in its then 20-year history.

Before the Scandinavian invasion of the rally scene, British drivers enjoyed at least as much success as those of other nations. In more recent times, only Midlander Roger Clark has been able to beat the Scandinavians at their own game with any consistency, usually driving a Ford Escort. However, it was a Scotsman, Andrew Cowan (in a Hillman

Hunter) who won the London-to-Sydney Marathon in 1967, an event led up to three-quarters distance by Clark.

Frenchmen, Germans, Italians, Dutchmen, East Africans (such as Shekhar Mehta and the brothers Joginder and Jaswant Singh), the Pole Sobiesław Zasada and men of many other nations have competed with distinction in a sport which takes place in most parts of the world.

Wherever the events are held, it is often one of the established 'stars' who wins, as the car-exporting manufacturers who value rallying as a major publicity exercise often support local events in far-flung lands by sending along their top-level crews. Very frequently, they find themselves competing against highly competent rivals who could certainly acquit themselves well in the major events of the European Rally Championship, given the opportunity with the right sort of machinery and sufficient experience to make use of it.

While the drivers get most of the publicity, their co-drivers or navigators play a vital part in the success of their efforts and, in this category, the British continue to perform with exceptional skill, with John Davenport and Henry Liddon in particular being worthy of mention.

Rallycross and Autocross

Rallycross and autocross events can be likened to racing in rally cars. They are rather like special stages run round a closed circuit and with direct competition between groups of competing cars. Depending on the course, cars can be started in groups (perhaps four at a time) or they may be sent off at intervals so that up to three or four competitors are competing on the circuit at the same time but are unlikely to pass each other.

The autocross is usually a summer event and has

Rallycross is racing on a rough surfaced circuit. Depicted is a European Championship round at Lydden Hill, Kent

resulted in the development of a particular type of car, of which the most successful in recent years has been John Bevan's Naveb, but the majority of competitors continue to use ordinary saloon vehicles. Some of the less ambitious even employ their own road transport, but the majority now keep a particular car for this branch of the sport alone.

Although cars may start in groups, autocrosses are normally events run against the stopwatch or a timing device, so that the entire entry can be related to each other.

While run mostly at local level, autocross events frequently qualify for regional or even national championships, but few competitors regard it as more than an amateur sport with the main object being to enjoy themselves. Rallycross, on the other hand, has become a largely professional pastime as this variation grew specifically out of the demand of television, and a high proportion of the events are staged for this purpose. There is a European championship which has attracted full-scale factory support, with both Ford and British Leyland building special 4-wheel-drive versions of production saloons, while Ford-engined Dafs and Porsche-engined Volkswagens are among the specialized vehicles which have been highly successful. There are front-wheel drive Minis, rear-engined Volks-wagens and front-engined rear-wheel-drive Fords. These are near-equal in this sport which can be highly spectacular although, in its more intense forms, somewhat rough and there is little regard for the other man's car given by many competitors.

Sporting and Production Car Trials

Trials in their modern sense are motor competitions in which drivers try to get their cars to surmount difficult tests up steep and slippery hills.

There are two main types of event called 'sporting' and 'production', the former being for specialized vehicles designed purely for the sport, while, as the name implies, the latter are for production models with little or no modification allowed.

The sporting trial car, although very carefully designed to achieve quite remarkable feats of adhesion and an ability to climb what look quite impossible inclines, is essentially a cheap form of vehicle, at least at the present time. Special cars can be bought for as little as £300–£400 and the sport can be enjoyed at almost any time of the year, particularly in mid-winter.

Production car trials are organized for four different types of vehicles: front-engined production saloons with front-wheel-drive, front-engined production saloons with rear-wheel-drive, front-engined rear-wheel-drive production sports cars, and rear-engined production cars and front-engined cars with a torque-biasing differential as catalogued for the car (this fourth category existing essentially as a result of the remarkable success in production car trials of Daf cars with their unique type of transmission).

Providing organizers choose their venues sensibly, so that the course is non-damaging, production car trials are as cheap for the competitor as are sporting car trials, perhaps even more so as the majority of competitors use nothing different from their normal road transport.

In either type of event the marking is based on a series of points corresponding to positions up the test so that if a section is divided into, say, twelve stages, a competitor will be penalized with a loss of points corresponding to his position if he stops part of the way up the stages of the section; if he stops halfway up he loses six points.

Hillclimbs, Sprints and other speed events, including Drag Racing

Speed events are a simple form of racing, but instead of competitors running against each other, they are competing against time alone. The earliest speed events were straightforward speed trials, these being contests to prove the pure performance of cars in a straight line. In the very early days, hills formed a special challenge and, initially, the most important part of the contest was just to surmount the hill, quite apart from doing so in the shortest time possible. That hurdle having been taken, the speed hillclimb soon developed into a competition

Remarkable traction up steep and slippery hills is the essence of the sporting trial car

form of its own and special courses were soon selected. These, while testing the ability of the car and driver to reach the top in the shortest time possible, also provided an extra test of skill to negotiate difficult bends and, ideally, could provide good viewing for spectators to enjoy the sport.

Hillclimbing is undoubtedly a satisfying sport for the driver, though these days, there is never any doubt that the car, always providing it is running decently, will surmount the hill. There is a subconscious feeling of achievement in conquering height, and hillclimbing in a car has a latent sense of safety combined with speed as, however difficult the corners may be, it always seems less hazardous than speeding downhill!

Hillclimbing has become highly organized in various parts of the world and is probably at its best in Europe, where famous hillclimbing courses such as that at Freiburg in Germany (6.928 miles/ 11.15 km), Mont Ventoux in France (13.422 miles/ 21.6 km) and Trento-Bondone in Italy (10.75 miles/ 17.2 km), have been established for many years and present a tremendous challenge to the driver and his car, rising to substantial heights and covering a great variety of corners.

Events such as these qualify for the European Hillclimb Championship which attracts its own strong following of competitors, some of whom take part in no other form of motoring competition. In the United Kingdom, because there are no substantial mountain ranges, the hillclimb courses tend to be very much shorter, mostly about a mile (1.6 km) or even less. Some of them, however, notably Shelsley Walsh in Worcestershire and Prescott in Gloucestershire, have been established since the early days of motoring sport, and are now well organized for the benefit of competitors and spectators alike. Even though its hills may be shorter, the UK hillclimbing competition is extensive and there are several championships, keenly fought by large numbers of competitors who enjoy a sport which remains almost wholly amateur but nonetheless keenly competitive. The typical hillclimb entry varies from quite ordinary small saloons to specialized racing cars using Formula 1 or Formula 5000 type engines, and 15 or even 20 different classes may be contested in a single day's racing, with cars timed electronically and running very rapidly one after another so that interest is sustained throughout the entire day.

Closely allied to hillclimbs are sprint events which differ mainly in being held on mostly flat courses, sometimes employing existing motor racing circuits. Frequently the entire lap may not be used but only the more twisty part of a course. Once again, a wide variety of cars compete and, in the UK, there are a number of championships which competitors can contest throughout a season.

At a number of venues, of which Brighton on the coast in Sussex is the best known, the original type of speed trial is still held, this being a simple sprint in a straight line usually over a measured kilometre or mile. An obvious development of this is drag racing, conducted over a $\frac{1}{4}$-mile (0.4 km) straight. Although this is an obvious development of the speed trial which is as old as the motor car, drag racing is, in fact, a relatively new development. It owes its origins to elicit street racing in the USA where authorities became perturbed at the number of accidents caused by over-enthusiastic young men racing against each other from a standing start up the street of a township. To harness their enthusiasm, the culprits were invited to leave the streets and to compete legally on private courses. From this humble beginning developed the highly organized drag race sport which now takes place throughout the USA and in various other venues in the world, including several in the UK. The best known of these is the so-called 'Santa-Pod', near Poddington in Northamptonshire, while both the Silverstone and Snetterton motor racing circuits now incorporate drag strips.

Again, all types of car can compete, but the sport has developed a particular type of sprint machine which is undoubtedly the fastest accelerating sort of car ever built, capable of achieving over 200 mph (321 kmh) at the end of the $\frac{1}{4}$-mile (0.4-km) strip and covering the distance in around 6 seconds. The fastest cars use heavily supercharged American-type engines of up to 8 litres capacity. They run on alcohol- and oxygen-bearing fuels such as nitromethane so that power outputs in the region of 2,000 horsepower have been achieved. Huge tyres of very soft rubber are used to harness this power. The drivers have to wear gas-masks to avoid breathing in dangerous fumes from their cars' exhaust systems while, at the end of the timed run, the cars are arrested by parachute as well as the somewhat ineffective rear brakes. An elaborate preparation system known as a 'burn-out' is used to prepare the tyres for maximum stickiness to ensure the extraordinary level of acceleration which is achieved.

Stock Car and Midget Car Racing

Although not normally recognized by the competitors in the more widely accepted forms of motor sport, and governed by bodies which do not come within the jurisdiction of the FIA, the CSI, and the national automobile clubs such as Great Britain's RAC, there are various other forms of racing which are properly organized and have their own regulating bodies. Stock car racing employs cars which are anything but the normally accepted idea of being 'stock' vehicles, as they are almost entirely specially-built cars. In certain classes a production body-shell (normally rescued from a breaker's yard) is used, but with the doors welded up, the windows removed and the structure reinforced with steel tubing. This prevents its collapse in the inevitable overturning incident which is part of the regular and popular spectator attraction of this form of motor sport. Unlike most other forms of motor racing, the fastest competitors are started from the back and are expected to fight their way through the entire field before going into the lead. Systems vary with different promoters, but this sport is now sufficiently lucrative that even the most novice type of competitor will normally be expected to come somewhere near breaking even financially at quite an early stage in his or her racing career. Stock car racing takes place frequently at motorcycle speedway tracks, but may be seen as well on some parts of established motor racing circuits and at various other special venues.

Midget racing also takes place on special short oval tracks, often loose-surfaced, and this is more closely akin to conventional motor racing, although the controlling bodies are not the normally recognized ones. The cars are professionally designed and built as small single-seater racing cars using well-tuned developments of small production car engines. A recent development has been the Super-Midget car, using $3\frac{1}{2}$-litre V8 engines which provide extra power and spectacle.

In some parts of the country, there is also 'Jalopy' racing, which normally takes place on any suitable farmer's field. This is mostly without proper background organization and sometimes with minimal spectator protection, so that, while drivers in stock car and midget racing car events are able to compete without incurring the wrath of those in charge of conventional racing, any recognized racing driver taking part in a jalopy event would be liable to have his competition licence for conventional events taken away from him.

Karting

Called 'Go-Kart Racing' in its early days, karting started in the USA and now has a widespread and enthusiastic following in many parts of the world. In recent years, it has produced many of the fastest and more successful young racing drivers at the very peak of their profession, notably the 1972 and 1974 world champion Emerson Fittipaldi of Brazil and the brilliant Swedish driver, Ronnie Peterson.

Karting is motor racing in miniature and it is possible for a driver to start at a very early age so that he can be a kart champion while still in his early teens. International championships are organized with remarkable speeds achieved by using karts having engines of only 100 cc while, in Great Britain, there is also a thriving class for karts with 250 cc engines and with multiple gears so that they lap full-scale motor racing circuits at speeds roughly equal to those achieved by 1,600 cc Formula Ford racing cars.

Some attempts have been made to employ streamlining but the most successful kart exponents tend to sit out in the open, wearing motorcycle racing leathers to provide some body protection, as well as using racing motorcycle engines as their means of propulsion. It is notable that a 250 cc kart is usually quicker round a circuit than a 250 cc solo racing motorcycle. This is because cornering speeds are incredibly high and are achieved with the same sort of four-wheel-drift as is used by drivers of the most powerful Grand Prix cars, hence the rapid transition to car racing which is frequently achieved by kart drivers.

Record-breaking

One of the most highly publicized forms of motor sport is record-breaking, particularly in those periods when attempts are being made on what is now called the World Land Speed Record, an occupation which reached the peak of its popularity in the 1920s and 1930s. It was resumed recently in the USA when, in particular, car constructors were able to obtain, second-hand and at low cost, immensely powerful surplus military aircraft gas-turbine engines. When mounted in a land vehicle they have achieved speeds of around 600 mph (965 kmh).

World speed record-breaking became recognized before the turn of the century when there was a great duel between two Frenchmen, the Comte de Chasseloup Laubat and Camille Jenatzy who, using electric cars, raised the record from 39 mph (62 kmh) to over 65 mph (104 kmh). In the twentieth century the great names have included the Hon. Charles Rolls, Henry Ford, Kenelm Lee Guinness, Sir Malcolm Campbell, Sir Henry Segrave, J. G. Parry Thomas, the American Ray Keech, Captain George Eyston, John Cobb and, in post-war years, Donald Campbell and the Americans Mickey Thompson, Craig Breedlove and Art Arfons, between them signify the transition between the original understanding that, to break the record, a car had to be driven through at least two of its wheels, to the current situation which requires the vehicle to run on wheels but not necessarily to be propelled through them. Thus it is permissible to build a body round an aircraft gas-turbine engine or a rocket and propel it along the chosen course. The wheels merely keep it on the surface and provide it with directional control.

Initially, records were broken on public highways and race tracks, but speeds rose and it became necessary to seek other venues. The last record to be established on a race track was K. Lee Guinness's 133.75 mph (215.24 kmh) in a Sunbeam at Brooklands in 1922. From then on the normal venue was a stretch of sand on the seashore initially at places such as Southport, Lancashire, or Pendine in Carmarthenshire. When the six-mile (9.6-km) stretch of sand at the latter venue became too short, the scene switched to Daytona Beach in the USA where Sir Malcolm Campbell achieved 276.82 mph (445.49 kmh) in 1935, using one of his Bluebirds. Since Daytona Beach on the Florida coastline proved inadequate, the most likely venue has been at Bonneville Salt Lake, in Utah, USA. A notable exception was when Donald Campbell went to a similar salt lake in the middle of Australia for his eventual successful attempt to exceed 400 mph (643 kmh) in the last Bluebird (which, although powered by a gas turbine, transmitted its power through the wheels).

In addition to the land speed record, the sport of record-breaking makes provision for every other conceivable class of vehicle, both in straight lines and round banked circuits. Records can be established over distances such as 1 kilometre, 1 mile, 10, 100 and 1,000 or even 10,000 miles or kilometres and for days and even weeks. Some drivers devote their lives to record-breaking as did Donald Campbell and George Eyston but, in many cases, the constructors of the record-breaking cars have entrusted the driving to those drivers recognized for their abilities in races, etc., so that the record books over the years have been full of such names as Rudolf Caracciola, Bernd Rosemeyer and, more recently, Stirling Moss and Phil Hill. To such men, any form of motor sport is a challenge which must be accepted.

INDEX

Numbers in italics indicate illustrations in the text